Letts
gets you through

AQA A-LEVEL
ENGLISH LITERATURE B
PRACTICE TEST PAPERS

PAUL BURNS

Contents

Acknowledgements

The author and publisher are grateful to the copyright holders for permission to use quoted materials and images.

Cover and page 1: © Shutterstock.com/Napat

Every effort has been made to trace copyright holders and obtain their permission for the use of copyright material. The author and publisher will gladly receive information enabling them to rectify any error or omission in subsequent editions. All facts are correct at time of going to press.

Published by Letts Educational
An imprint of HarperCollins*Publishers*
1 London Bridge Street
London SE1 9GF
ISBN: 9780008276225

First published 2018

10 9 8 7 6 5 4 3 2 1

© HarperCollins*Publishers* Limited 2018

All rights reserved. No part of this publication may be reproduced, stored in a retrieval system, or transmitted, in any form or by any means, electronic, mechanical, photocopying, recording or otherwise, without the prior permission of Letts Educational.

British Library Cataloguing in Publication Data.

A CIP record of this book is available from the British Library.

Commissioning Editor: Gillian Bowman
Author: Paul Burns
Project Management: Mark Steward
Copyediting: Louise Robb
Proof checking: Rachel Hamar
Cover Design: Sarah Duxbury
Inside Concept Design: Ian Wrigley
Text Design and Layout: Jouve India
Production: Natalia Rebow
Printed by CPI Group (UK) Ltd, Croydon CR0 4YY

With thanks to Lauren Palmer for her contribution to Exam 1, Papers 1A, 2A and 2B, and Exam 2, Paper 1A.

Page 18, Copyright ©Truman Capote, 1965. Reproduced by permission of Penguin Books Ltd. Page 24, *Nineteen Eighty-Four* by George Orwell (Copyright© George Orwell1 1949) Reproduced by permission of Bill Hamilton as the Literary Executor of the Estate of the Late Sonia Brownell Orwell.

Practice Exam 1

A-Level

ENGLISH LITERATURE B

Paper 1A: Literary Genres: Aspects of Tragedy

Time allowed: 2 hours 30 minutes

Instructions

- Use black ink or black ball point pen.
- There are three sections: A, B and C.
- Answer **one** question from Section A, **one** from Section B and **one** from Section C.
- You may answer on the same Shakespeare play in Sections A and B.
- For Section C, you must write about **two** texts: **one** drama text and **one** further text, **one** of which must be written pre-1900.
- Write down all of rough work. Cross through any work that you do not want to be marked.

Information

- The maximum mark for this paper is 75.
- The marks for questions are shown in brackets.
- There are 25 marks for Question 1, 25 marks for Question 2 and 25 marks for Question 3

- You will be marked on your ability to:
  - use good English
  - organise information clearly
  - use specialist vocabulary where appropriate.

- In your response you need to:
  - analyse carefully the writers' methods
  - explore the contexts of the texts you are writing about
  - explore connections across the texts you have studied
  - explore different interpretations of your texts.

Section A

Answer **one** question in this section.

EITHER

[0][1] *Othello* – William Shakespeare

Read the extract below and answer the question.

Explore the significance of this extract in relation to the tragedy of the play as a whole.

Remember to include in your answer relevant analysis of Shakespeare's dramatic methods.

[25 marks]

EMILIA
> I have laid those sheets you bade me on the bed.

DESDEMONA
> All's one. Good faith, how foolish are our minds!
> If I do die before thee prithee, shroud me
> In one of those same sheets.

EMILIA
> Come, come you talk.

DESDEMONA
> My mother had a maid call'd Barbary:
> She was in love, and he she loved proved mad
> And did forsake her: she had a song of 'willow';
> An old thing 'twas, but it express'd her fortune,
> And she died singing it: that song to-night
> Will not go from my mind; I have much to do,
> But to go hang my head all at one side,
> And sing it like poor Barbary. Prithee, dispatch.

EMILIA
> Shall I go fetch your night-gown?

DESDEMONA
> No, unpin me here.
> This Lodovico is a proper man.

EMILIA
> A very handsome man.

DESDEMONA
> He speaks well.

EMILIA
> I know a lady in Venice would have walked barefoot
> to Palestine for a touch of his nether lip.

DESDEMONA
> *[Singing]* The poor soul sat sighing by a sycamore tree,
> Sing all a green willow:

Her hand on her bosom, her head on her knee,
Sing willow, willow, willow:
The fresh streams ran by her, and murmur'd her moans;
Sing willow, willow, willow;
Her salt tears fell from her, and soften'd the stones;
Lay by these:-
(Singing)
Sing willow, willow, willow;
Prithee, hie thee; he'll come anon:-
Sing all a green willow must be my garland.
Let nobody blame him; his scorn I approve,-
Nay, that's not next.- Hark! Who is't that knocks?

EMILIA

It is the wind.

DESDEMONA

[Singing] I call'd my love false love; but what
said he then?
Sing willow, willow, willow:
If I court moe women, you'll couch with moe men!
So, get thee gone; good night: mine eyes do itch;
Doth that bode weeping?

EMILIA

'Tis neither here nor there.

DESDEMONA

I have heard it said so. O, these men, these men!
Dost thou in conscience think - tell me, Emilia,-
That there be women do abuse their husbands
In such gross kind?

(Act 4, Scene 3)

OR

0 2   *King Lear* – **William Shakespeare**

Read the extract below and answer the question.

Explore the significance of this extract in relation to the tragedy of the play as a whole.

Remember to include in your answer relevant analysis of Shakespeare's dramatic methods.

[25 marks]

KING LEAR

Meantime we shall express our darker purpose.
Give me the map there. Know that we have divided
In three our kingdom: and 'tis our fast intent
To shake all cares and business from our age;

Conferring them on younger strengths, while we
Unburthen'd crawl toward death. Our son of Cornwall,
And you, our no less loving son of Albany,
We have this hour a constant will to publish
Our daughters' several dowers, that future strife
May be prevented now. The princes, France and Burgundy,
Great rivals in our youngest daughter's love,
Long in our court have made their amorous sojourn,
And here are to be answer'd. Tell me, my daughters,-
Since now we will divest us both of rule,
Interest of territory, cares of state,-
Which of you shall we say doth love us most?
That we our largest bounty may extend
Where nature doth with merit challenge. Goneril,
Our eldest-born, speak first.

GONERIL

Sir, I love you more than words can wield the matter;
Dearer than eye-sight, space, and liberty;
Beyond what can be valued, rich or rare;
No less than life, with grace, health, beauty, honour;
As much as child e'er loved, or father found;
A love that makes breath poor, and speech unable;
Beyond all manner of so much I love you.

CORDELIA

[Aside] What shall Cordelia do?
Love, and be silent.

KING LEAR

Of all these bounds, even from this line to this,
With shadowy forests and with champains rich'd,
With plenteous rivers and wide-skirted meads,
We make thee lady: to thine and Albany's issue
Be this perpetual. What says our second daughter,
Our dearest Regan, wife to Cornwall? Speak.

REGAN

Sir, I am made
Of the self-same metal that my sister is,
And prize me at her worth. In my true heart
I find she names my very deed of love;
Only she comes too short: that I profess
Myself an enemy to all other joys,
Which the most precious square of sense possesses;
And find I am alone felicitate
In your dear highness' love.

CORDELIA

[Aside] Then poor Cordelia!
And yet not so; since, I am sure, my love's
More ponderous than my tongue.

KING LEAR
    To thee and thine hereditary ever
    Remain this ample third of our fair kingdom;
    No less in space, validity, and pleasure,
    Than that conferr'd on Goneril. Now, our joy,
    Although the last, not least; to whose young love
    The vines of France and milk of Burgundy
    Strive to be interess'd; what can you say to draw
    A third more opulent than your sisters? Speak.

CORDELIA
    Nothing, my lord.

KING LEAR
    Nothing!

CORDELIA
    Nothing.

KING LEAR
    Nothing will come of nothing: speak again.

(Act 1, Scene 1)

Section B

Answer **one** question in this section.

EITHER

0 3   *Othello* – **William Shakespeare**

'Desdemona's tragedy is more profound and lamentable than her husband's.'

To what extent do you agree with this view?

Remember to include in your answer relevant comment on Shakespeare's dramatic methods.

[25 marks]

OR

0 4   *Othello* – **William Shakespeare**

'The tragedy of the play is caused by the trust characters place in appearances rather than the reality of the situations they are in.'

To what extent do you agree with this view?

Remember to include in your answer relevant comment on Shakespeare's dramatic methods.

[25 marks]

OR

0 5   *King Lear* – **William Shakespeare**

'Madness is the essence of the tragedy in *King Lear*; the play is an examination of the danger of madness in a monarch.'

To what extent do you agree with this view?

Remember to include in your answer relevant comment on Shakespeare's dramatic methods.

[25 marks]

OR

0 6   *King Lear* – **William Shakespeare**

'The Fool is the most enlightened character within the play, offering insight and reflection for Lear and the audience.'

To what extent do you agree with this view?

Remember to include in your answer relevant comment on Shakespeare's dramatic methods.

[25 marks]

Section C

Answer **one** question in this section.

In this section you must write about **two** texts. **One** text must be a drama text.

One text must be written pre-1900. You can write about the following texts:

Richard II (pre-1900 drama)
Death of a Salesman (drama)
Tess of the D'Urbervilles (pre-1900)
The Great Gatsby
Keats Poetry Selection (pre-1900)
Poetry Anthology: Tragedy (at least **two** poems must be covered).

EITHER

| 0 | 7 | 'Tragedies will always leave readers satisfied. The pain and suffering of the characters allows catharsis for readers and audiences.'

To what extent do you agree with this view in relation to **two** texts you have studied?

Remember to include in your answer relevant comment on the ways the writers have shaped meanings.

[25 marks]

OR

| 0 | 8 | 'Readers and audiences often feel less sympathy for tragic heroes than for those affected by their actions.'

To what extent do you agree with this view in relation to **two** texts you have studied?

Remember to include in your answer relevant comment on the ways the writers have shaped meanings.

[25 marks]

Name: ....

Practice Exam 1
A-Level
ENGLISH LITERATURE B
Paper 1B: Literary Genres: Aspects of Comedy

Time allowed: 2 hours 30 minutes

Instructions
- Use black ink or black ball point pen.
- There are three sections: A, B and C.
- Answer **one** question from Section A, **one** from Section B and **one** from Section C.
- You may answer on the same Shakespeare play in Sections A and B.
- For Section C, you must write about **two** texts: **one** pre-1900 drama text and **one** further text
- Write down all of rough work. Cross through any work that you do not want to be marked.

Information
- The maximum mark for this paper is 75.
- The marks for questions are shown in brackets.
- There are 25 marks for Question 1, 25 marks for Question 2 and 25 marks for Question 3

- You will be marked on your ability to:
  - use good English
  - organise information clearly
  - use specialist vocabulary where appropriate.
- In your response you need to:
  - analyse carefully the writers' methods
  - explore the contexts of the texts you are writing about
  - explore connections across the texts you have studied

Section A

Answer **one** question in this section.

EITHER

0 1 *The Taming of the Shrew* – William Shakespeare

Read the extract below and answer the question.

Explore the significance of this extract in relation to the comedy of the play as a whole.

Remember to include in your answer relevant analysis of Shakespeare's dramatic methods.

[25 marks]

TRANIO
Let us entreat you stay till after dinner.

PETRUCHIO
It may not be.

GREMIO
Let me entreat you.

PETRUCHIO
It cannot be.

KATHERINA
Let me entreat you.

PETRUCHIO
I am content.

KATHERINA
Are you content to stay?

PETRUCHIO
I am content you shall entreat me stay –
But yet not stay, entreat me how you can.

KATHERINA
Now, if you love me, stay.

PETRUCHIO
Grumio, my horse!

GRUMIO
Ay, sir, they be ready – the oats have eaten the horses.

KATHERINA
Nay then,
Do what thou canst. I will not go today!
No, nor tomorrow – not till I please myself.
The door is open, sir, there lies your way;
You may be jogging whiles your boots are green.
For me, I'll not be gone till I please myself.
'Tis like you'll prove a jolly surly groom
That take it on you at the first so roundly.

PETRUCHIO

O Kate, content thee; prithee be not angry.

KATHERINA

I will be angry. Why hast thou to do? –
Father, be quiet. He shall stay my leisure.

GREMIO

Ay, marry, sir, now it begins to work.

KATHERINA

Gentlemen, forward to the bridal dinner.
I see a woman may be made a fool
If she had not a spirit to resist.

PETRUCHIO

They shall go forward, Kate, at thy command.
Obey the bride, you that attend on her.
Go to the feast, revel and domineer,
Carouse full measure to her maidenhead,
Be mad and merry – or go hang yourselves,
But for my bonny Kate, she must with me.
Nay, look not big, nor stamp, nor stare, nor fret;
I will be master of what is mine own.
She is my goods, my chattels; she is my house,
My household-stuff, my field, my barn,
My horse, my ox, my ass, my anything,
And here she stands. Touch her whoever dare,
I'll bring mine action on the proudest he
That stops my way in Padua. Grumio,
Draw forth thy weapon – We are beset with thieves!
Rescue thy mistress, if thou be man.–
Fear not, sweet wench, they shall not touch thee, Kate;
I'll buckler thee against a million!

Exeunt Petruchio, Katherina [and Grumio]

BAPTISTA

Nay, let them go – a couple of quiet ones!

GREMIO

Went they not quickly, I should die laughing.

TRANIO

Of all mad matches never was the like.

(Act 3, Scene 2)

OR

0 2 *Twelfth Night* – **William Shakespeare**

Read the extract below and answer the question.

Explore the significance of this extract in relation to the comedy of the play as a whole.

Remember to include in your answer relevant analysis of Shakespeare's dramatic methods.

[25 marks]

MARIA

What a caterwauling do you keep here? If my lady have not called up her steward Malvolio and bid him turn you out of doors, never trust me.

SIR TOBY

My lady's a Cataian, we are politicians, Malvolio's a Peg-a-Ramsey, and [*sings*] 'Three merry me be we.' Am not I consanguineous? Am I not of her blood? Tilly vally! 'Lady!' [*Sings*] 'There dwelt a man in Babylon, lady, lady.'

FESTE

Beshrew me the knight's in admirable fooling.

SIR ANDREW

Ay, he does well enough if he be disposed, and so do I, too; he does it with a better grace, but I do it more natural.

SIR TOBY

[*Sings*] O' the twelfth day of December –

MARIA

For the love o'God, peace!
        Enter MALVOLIO

MALVOLIO

My masters, are you mad? Or what are you? Have you no wit, manners, nor honesty but to gabble like tinkers at this time of night? Do ye make an alehouse of my lady's house, that ye squeak out your coziers' catches without any mitigation or remorse of voice? Is there no respect of place, persons, nor time in you?

SIR TOBY

We did keep time, sir, in our catches. Sneck up!

MALVOLIO

Sir Toby, I must be round with you. My lady bade me tell you that, though she harbours you as her kinsman, she's nothing allied to your disorders. If you can separate yourself and your misdemeanours, you are welcome to the house; if not, and it would please you to take leave of her, she is very willing to bid you farewell.

SIR TOBY

[*Sings*] Farewell, dear heart, since I must needs be gone.

MARIA

Nay, good Sir Toby.

SIR TOBY

[*Sings*] His eyes do show his days are almost done.

MALVOLIO

Is't even so?

SIR TOBY

But I will never die.

FESTE

[*Sings*] Sir Toby, there you lie.

MALVOLIO

This is much credit to you.

SIR TOBY

[*Sings*] Shall I bid him go?

FESTE

[*Sings*] What and if you do?

SIR TOBY

[*Sings*] Shall I bid him go, and spare not?

FESTE

[*Sings*] O no, no, no, no, you dare not.

SIR TOBY

Out o'time, sir? Ye lie! Art any more than a steward? Dost thou think that because thou art virtuous there shall be no more cakes and ale?

FESTE

Yes, by St Anne, and ginger shall be hot i'th'mouth too.

[Exit]

SIR TOBY

Th'art i'th'right. Go, sir, rub your chain with crumbs. A stoup of wine, Maria!

MALVOLIO

Mistress Mary, if you prized my lady's favour at anything more than contempt, you would not give means for this uncivil rule; she shall know of it by this hand.

Exit

(Act 2, Scene 3)

Section B

Answer **one** question in this section.

EITHER

| 0 | 3 | **The Taming of the Shrew – William Shakespeare**

'*The Taming of the Shrew* creates comedy by demonstrating that in the war of the sexes men will always be the winners.'

To what extent do you agree with this view?

Remember to include in your answer relevant comment on Shakespeare's dramatic methods.

[25 marks]

OR

| 0 | 4 | **The Taming of the Shrew – William Shakespeare**

'*The Taming of the Shrew* is about two imperfect people who find true love with each other.'

To what extent do you agree with this view?

Remember to include in your answer relevant comment on Shakespeare's dramatic methods.

[25 marks]

OR

| 0 | 5 | **Twelfth Night – William Shakespeare**

'In *Twelfth Night* love is shown to be a form of comic madness.'

To what extent do you agree with this view?

Remember to include in your answer relevant comment on Shakespeare's dramatic methods.

[25 marks]

OR

| 0 | 6 | **Twelfth Night – William Shakespeare**

'Viola refers to disguise as "a wickedness" but in *Twelfth Night* disguise is ultimately a force for good.'

To what extent do you agree with this view?

Remember to include in your answer relevant comment on Shakespeare's dramatic methods.

[25 marks]

Section C

Answer **one** question in this section

In this section you must write about **two** texts, one of which must be a pre-1900 drama text.

You can write about the following texts:

She Stoops to Conquer (pre-1900 drama)
The Importance of Being Earnest (pre-1900 drama)
Emma
Small Island
The Nun's Priest's Tale
Poetry Anthology: Comedy

EITHER

0 7   'All the best comedy is cruel.'

To what extent do you agree with this view in relation to **two** texts you have studied?

Remember to include in your answer relevant comment on the ways the writers have shaped meanings.

[25 marks]

OR

0 8   'Comedic literature must end with a sense that all's right with the world, however unlikely that might seem in view of what has gone before.'

To what extent do you agree with this view in relation to **two** texts you have studied?

Remember to include in your answer relevant comment on the ways the writers have shaped meanings.

[25 marks]

Practice Exam 1

A-Level

ENGLISH LITERATURE B

Paper 2A: Texts and Genres: Elements of Crime Writing

Time allowed: 3 hours

Materials

For this paper you must have:
- a copy of the set text(s) you have studied for Section B and Section C. These texts must not be annotated and must not contain additional notes or materials.

Instructions
- Use black ink or black ball point pen.
- There are three sections: A, B and C.
- You must answer the question in Section A, **one** question from Section B and **one** question from Section C. Over Section B and Section C, you must write about **three** texts: at least **one** poetry text, **one** post-2000 prose text and **one** further text.

Information
- The maximum mark for this paper is 75.
- The marks for questions are shown in brackets.

- You will be marked on your ability to:
  - use good English
  - organise information clearly
  - use specialist vocabulary where appropriate.
- In your response you need to:
  - analyse carefully the writers' methods
  - explore the contexts of the texts you are writing about
  - explore connections across the texts you have studied
  - Explore different interpretations of your texts

Section A

Answer the question in this section

0 1 Explore the significance of elements of crime writing in this extract. Remember to include in your answer relevant detailed analysis of the ways the author has shaped meanings.

[25 marks]

This extract is taken from Truman Capote's novel *In Cold Blood* (published 1966). It is a 'non-fiction novel' detailing the 1959 murders of 4 members of the Herbert Clutter family in the small farming town of Holcomb, Kansas. Whilst travelling to Holcomb to commit the murders, Dick and Perry stop for food and gas, and Dick thinks about the planned murders and his partnership with Perry while Perry has shut himself in the bathroom to take aspirin.

Dick dropped a dime in a vending machine, pulled the lever, and picked up a bag of jelly beans; munching, he wandered back to the car and lounged there watching the young attendant's efforts to rid the windshield of Kansas dust and the slime of battered insects. The attendant, whose name was James Spor, felt uneasy. Dick's eyes and sullen expression and Perry's strange, prolonged sojourn in the lavatory disturbed him. (The next day, he reported to his employer, "We had some tough customers in here last night," but he did not think, then or for the longest while, to connect the visitors with the tragedy in Holcomb.)

Dick said, "Kind of slow around here."

"Sure is," James Spor said. "You're the only body stopped here since two hours. Where you coming from?"

"Kansas City."

"Here to hunt?'

"Just passing through. On our way to Arizona. We got jobs waiting there. Construction work. Any idea the mileage between here and Tucumcari, New Mexico?"

"Can't say I do. Three dollars six cents." He accepted Dick's money, made change, and said, "You'll excuse me, sir? I'm doing a job. Putting a bumper on a truck."

Dick waited, ate some jelly beans, impatiently gunned the motor, sounded the horn. Was it possible that he had misjudged Perry's character? That Perry, of all people, was suffering a sudden case of "blood bubbles"? A year ago, when they first encountered each other, he'd thought Perry "a good guy," if a bit "stuck on himself," "sentimental," too much "the dreamer." He had liked him but not considered him especially worth cultivating until, one day, Perry described a murder, telling how, simply for "the hell of it," he had killed a colored man in Las Vegas—beaten him to death with a bicycle chain. The anecdote elevated Dick's opinion of Little Perry; he began to see more of him, and, like Willie-Jay, though for dissimilar reasons, gradually decided that Perry possessed unusual and valuable qualities. Several murderers, or men who boasted of murder or their willingness to commit it, circulated inside Lansing, but Dick became convinced that Perry was that rarity, "a natural killer"—absolutely sane, but conscienceless, and capable of dealing, with or without motive, the coldest-blooded deathblows. It was Dick's theory that such a gift could, under his supervision, be profitably exploited. Having reached this conclusion, he had proceeded to woo Perry, flatter him—pretend, for example, that he believed all the buried-treasure stuff and shared his beachcomber yearnings and seaport longings, none of which appealed to Dick, who wanted "a regular life," with a business of his own, a house, a horse to ride, a new car, and "plenty of blond chicken." It was important, however, that Perry not suspect this—not until Perry, with his gift, had helped further Dick's ambitions. But perhaps it was Dick who had miscalculated, been duped; if so—if it developed that Perry was, after all, only an "ordinary punk"—then "the party" was over, the months of planning were wasted, there was nothing to do but turn and go. It mustn't happen; Dick returned to the station.

The door to the men's room was still bolted. He banged on it: "For Christsake, Perry!"

"In a minute."

"What's the matter? You sick?"

Perry gripped the edge of the washbasin and hauled himself to a standing position. His legs trembled; the pain in his knees made him perspire. He wiped his face with a paper towel. He unlocked the door and said, "O.K. Let's go."

Over Section B and Section C, you must write about **three** texts from the following list. At least **one** must be a pre-1900 poetry text. At least **one** must be a post-2000 prose text:

Selected Poems: Crabbe, Browning and Wilde (pre-1900 poetry)
The Rime of the Ancient Mariner (pre-1900 poetry)
Atonement (post-2000 prose)
When Will There Be Good News? (post-2000 prose)
Oliver Twist
The Murder of Roger Ackroyd
Brighton Rock
Hamlet

Section B

Answer **one** question in this section.

EITHER

0 2   *Selected Poems* **– George Crabbe, Robert Browning and Oscar Wilde**

'In these poems our interest in the criminal is far greater than our sympathy for the victim.'

To what extent do you agree with this view? Remember to include in your answer relevant detailed exploration of the poets' authorial methods.

You should refer to the work of at least **two poets** in your answer.

[25 marks]

OR

0 3   *The Rime of the Ancient Mariner* **– Samuel Taylor Coleridge**

'Coleridge's poem explores all elements of the crime genre without any crimes ever being committed.'

To what extent do you agree with this view? Remember to include in your answer relevant detailed exploration of Coleridge's authorial methods.

[25 marks]

OR

0 4   *When Will There Be Good News?* **– Kate Atkinson**

'This novel is as much about the effects of love as it is about the effects of crime.'

To what extent do you agree with this view? Remember to include in your answer relevant detailed exploration of Atkinson's authorial methods.

[25 marks]

OR

0 5   *Atonement* – Ian McEwan

'The ending of the novel leaves readers satisfied that Briony has paid for her crime.'

To what extent do you agree with this view? Remember to include in your answer relevant detailed exploration of McEwan's authorial methods.

[25 marks]

OR

0 6   *Oliver Twist* – Charles Dickens

'Readers of Oliver Twist are left sympathetic to the lifestyle of the criminals portrayed.'

To what extent do you agree with this view? Remember to include in your answer relevant detailed exploration of Dickens's authorial methods.

[25 marks]

OR

0 7   *Brighton Rock* – Graham Greene

'Brighton Rock is an examination of the differences between religious morality and justice.'

To what extent do you agree with this view? Remember to include in your answer relevant detailed exploration of Greene's authorial methods.

[25 marks]

OR

0 8   *The Murder of Roger Ackroyd* – Agatha Christie

'*The Murder of Roger Ackroyd* is all about the revelation of the murderer: its success depends on the reader being satisfied with this revelation.'

To what extent do you agree with this view? Remember to include in your answer relevant detailed exploration of Christie's authorial methods.

[25 marks]

OR

0 9   *Hamlet* – William Shakespeare

'Any crimes committed in *Hamlet* are ultimately caused by appearance of the ghost.'

To what extent do you agree with this view? Remember to include in your answer relevant detailed exploration of Shakespeare's dramatic methods.

[25 marks]

Section C

Answer **one** question in this section.

In your answer you must write about **two** texts that you have **not** used in **Section B**.

EITHER

| 1 | 0 | 'Notions of sin and morality are the foundations of crime writing.'

Explore the significance of sin and morality in relation to crime in **two** of the texts you have studied.

[25 marks]

OR

| 1 | 1 | 'Themes of betrayal and secrecy are central to crime literature.'

Explore the significance of betrayal and secrets in **two** crime texts you have studied.

[25 marks]

Practice Exam 1
A-Level
ENGLISH LITERATURE B
Paper 2B: Texts and Genres: Elements of Political and Social Protest Writing

Time allowed: 3 hours

Materials

For this paper you must have:

- a copy of the set text(s) you have studied for Section B and Section C. These texts must not be annotated and must not contain additional notes or materials.

Instructions

- Use black ink or black ball point pen.
- There are three sections: A, B and C.
- You must answer the question in Section A, **one** question from Section B and **one** question from Section C. Over Section B and Section C, you must write about **three** texts: **one** poetry text, **one** post-2000 prose text and **one** further text. **One** of your texts must be written pre-1900.

Information

- The maximum mark for this paper is 75.
- The marks for questions are shown in brackets.

- You will be marked on your ability to:
  - use good English
  - organise information clearly
  - use specialist vocabulary where appropriate.
- In your response you need to:
  - analyse carefully the writers' methods
  - explore the contexts of the texts you are writing about
  - explore connections across the texts you have studied
  - Explore different interpretations of your texts

Section A

Answer the question in this section.

0 1 'Explore the significance of elements of social protest writing in this extract. Remember to include in your answer relevant detailed analysis of the ways the author has shaped meanings.

[25 marks]

This extract is taken from George Orwell's novel *1984* (published 1949). It is set in an alternative future where Great Britain has become a province of the super state Oceania. People in Oceania are all members of the English Socialist party (Ingsoc) and are governed by a ruler know as Big Brother. Here the narrator is explaining the nature of the Ingsoc party and how crimes are detected and punished within society.

A Party member lives from birth to death under the eye of the Thought Police. Even when he is alone he can never be sure that he is alone. Wherever he may be, asleep or awake, working or resting, in his bath or in bed, he can be inspected without warning and without knowing that he is being inspected. Nothing that he does is indifferent. His friendships, his relaxations, his behaviour toward his wife and children, the expression of his face when he is alone, the words he mutters in sleep, even the characteristic movements of his body, are all jealously scrutinized. Not only any actual misdemeanour, but any eccentricity, however small, any change of habits, any nervous mannerism that could possibly be the symptom of an inner struggle, is certain to be detected. He has no freedom of choice in any direction whatever.

On the other hand, his actions are not regulated by law or by any clearly formulated code of behaviour. In Oceania there is no law. Thoughts and actions which, when detected, mean certain death are not formally forbidden, and the endless purges, arrests, tortures, imprisonments, and vaporizations are not inflicted as punishment for crimes which have actually been committed, but are merely the wiping-out of persons who might perhaps commit a crime at some time in the future. A Party member is required to have not only the right opinions, but the right instincts. Many of the beliefs and attitudes demanded of him are never plainly stated, and could not be stated without laying bare the contradictions inherent in Ingsoc. If he is a person naturally orthodox (in Newspeak, a goodthinker), he will in all circumstances know, without taking thought, what is the true belief or the desirable emotion. But in any case an elaborate mental training, undergone in childhood and grouping itself round the Newspeak words crimestop, blackwhite, and doublethink, makes him unwilling and unable to think too deeply on any subject whatever.

A Party member is expected to have no private emotions and no respites from enthusiasm. He is supposed to live in a continuous frenzy of hatred of foreign enemies and internal traitors, triumph over victories, and self-abasement before the power and wisdom of the Party. The discontents produced by his bare, unsatisfying life are deliberately turned outwards and dissipated by such devices as the Two Minutes Hate, and the speculations which might possibly induce a sceptical or rebellious attitude are killed in advance by his early acquired inner discipline. The first and simplest stage in the discipline, which can be taught even to young children, is called, in Newspeak, crimestop. Crimestop means the faculty of stopping short, as though by instinct, at the threshold of any dangerous thought. It includes the power of not grasping analogies, of failing to perceive logical errors, of misunderstanding the simplest arguments if they are inimical to Ingsoc, and of being bored or repelled by any train of thought which is capable of leading in a heretical direction. Crimestop, in short, means protective stupidity. But stupidity is not enough. On the contrary, orthodoxy in the full sense demands a control over one's own mental processes as complete as that of a contortionist over his body. Oceanic society rests ultimately on the belief that Big Brother is omnipotent and that the Party is infallible. But since in reality Big Brother is not omnipotent and the Party is not infallible, there is need for an unwearying, moment-to-moment flexibility in the treatment of facts. The key word here is blackwhite. Like so many Newspeak words, this word has two mutually contradictory meanings. Applied to an opponent, it means the habit of impudently claiming that black is white, in contradiction of the plain facts. Applied to a Party member, it means a loyal willingness to say that black is white when Party discipline demands this. But it means also the ability to believe that black is white, and more, to know that black is white, and to forget that one has ever believed the contrary. This demands a continuous alteration of the past, made possible by the system of thought which really embraces all the rest, and which is known in Newspeak as doublethink.

Over **Section B** and **Section C**, you must write about **three** texts from the following list:

Songs of Innocence and of Experience (pre-1900)
Tony Harrison: *Selected Poems*
Harvest (post-2000 prose)
The Kite Runner (post-2000 prose)
A Doll's House (pre-1900)
Hard Times (pre-1900)
Henry IV Part 1 (pre-1900)
The Handmaid's Tale.

Choose **one** of the following combinations:

Songs of Innocence and Experience plus 1 post-2000 prose text plus 1 other text.
Tony Harrison: *Selected Poems* plus 1 post-2000 prose text plus 1 pre-1900 text.

Section B

Answer **one** question in this section

EITHER

| 0 | 2 | **Songs of Innocence and Experience – William Blake**

'Blake suggests that political and social influences are the greatest corruptors of human innocence.'

To what extent do you agree with this view? Remember to include in your answer relevant detailed exploration of Blake's authorial methods.

[25 marks]

OR

| 0 | 3 | **Selected Poems – Tony Harrison**

'Harrison's poems suggest that social class and education are the biggest segregators of modern society.'

To what extent do you agree with this view? Remember to include in your answer relevant detailed exploration of Harrison's authorial methods.

[25 marks]

OR

| 0 | 4 | **The Kite Runner – Kahled Hosseini**

'Hosseini's novel deals with class and gender struggles above those of ethnicity or culture.'

To what extent do you agree with this view? Remember to include in your answer relevant detailed exploration of Hosseini's authorial methods.

[25 marks]

OR

0 5   *Harvest* – Jim Crace

'*Harvest* is a warning about the dangers of isolationism in an industrial society.'

To what extent do you agree with this view? Remember to include in your answer relevant detailed exploration of Crace's authorial methods.

[25 marks]

OR

0 6   *Hard Times* – Charles Dickens

'In *Hard Times* Dickens shows that both the greatest failing and the greatest success of a society lie in its attitude to education.'

To what extent do you agree with this view? Remember to include in your answer relevant detailed exploration of Dickens' authorial methods.

[25 marks]

OR

0 7   *Henry IV Part 1* – William Shakespeare

'Those in the pursuit of power are often more dangerous than those who already possess it.'

To what extent do you agree with this view? Remember to include in your answer relevant detailed exploration of Shakespeare's dramatic methods.

[25 marks]

OR

0 8   *A Doll's House* – Henrik Ibsen (translated by Michael Meyer)

'Nora's powerlessness stems almost entirely from societal obsession with reputation and appearance.'

To what extent do you agree with this view of the play? Remember to include in your answer relevant detailed exploration of Ibsen's dramatic methods.

[25 marks]

OR

0 9   *The Handmaid's Tale* – Margaret Atwood

'The Handmaid's Tale is a novel primarily concerned with rebellion and not oppression.'

To what extent do you agree with this view? Remember to include in your answer relevant detailed exploration of Atwood's dramatic methods.

[25 marks]

Answer **one** question in this section.

In your answer you must write about **two** texts that you have **not** used in **Section B**.

EITHER

| 1 | 0 | 'The portrayal of oppression and servitude lies at the heart of political and social protest writing.'

Explore the significance of oppression and servitude as it is presented in **two** political and social protest texts you have studied.

[25 marks]

OR

| 1 | 1 | 'Political and social protest writing must always deal with issues of class and wealth above all other divisions.'

Explore the significance of class and wealth in **two** political and social protest texts you have studied.

[25 marks]

Practice Exam 2
A-Level
ENGLISH LITERATURE B
Paper 1A: Literary Genres: Aspects of Tragedy

Time allowed: 2 hours 30 minutes

Instructions

- Use black ink or black ball point pen.
- There are three sections: A, B and C.
- Answer **one** question from Section A, **one** from Section B and **one** from Section C.
- You may answer on the same Shakespeare play in Sections A and B.
- For Section C, you must write about **two** texts: **one** drama text and **one** further text, **one** of which must be written pre-1900.
- Write down all of rough work. Cross through any work that you do not want to be marked.

Information

- The maximum mark for this paper is 75.
- The marks for questions are shown in brackets.
- There are 25 marks for Question 1, 25 marks for Question 2 and 25 marks for Question 3

- You will be marked on your ability to:
  - use good English
  - organise information clearly
  - use specialist vocabulary where appropriate.

- In your response you need to:
  - analyse carefully the writers' methods
  - explore the contexts of the texts you are writing about
  - explore connections across the texts you have studied
  - explore different interpretations of your texts.

Answer **one** question in this section.

EITHER

| 0 1 | *Othello* – **William Shakespeare** |

Read the extract below and answer the question.

Explore the significance of this extract in relation to the tragedy of the play as a whole.

Remember to include in your answer relevant analysis of Shakespeare's dramatic methods.

[25 marks]

GRATIANO
    What is the matter?

OTHELLO
    Behold, I have a weapon;
    A better never did itself sustain
    Upon a soldier's thigh: I have seen the day,
    That, with this little arm and this good sword,
    I have made my way through more impediments
    Than twenty times your stop: but, O vain boast!
    Who can control his fate? 'Tis not so now.
    Be not afraid, though you do see me weapon'd;
    Here is my journey's end, here is my butt,
    And very sea-mark of my utmost sail.
    Do you go back dismay'd? 'Tis a lost fear;
    Man but a rush against Othello's breast,
    And he retires. Where should Othello go?
    Now, how dost thou look now? O ill-starr'd wench!
    Pale as thy smock! when we shall meet at compt,
    This look of thine will hurl my soul from heaven,
    And fiends will snatch at it. Cold, cold, my girl!
    Even like thy chastity. O cursed slave!
    Whip me, ye devils,
    From the possession of this heavenly sight!
    Blow me about in winds! roast me in sulphur!
    Wash me in steep-down gulfs of liquid fire!
    O Desdemona! Desdemona! dead!
    Oh! Oh! Oh!

Enter LODOVICO. MONTANO, CASSIO carried in a chair, and Officers with IAGO, prisoner

LODOVICO
    Where is this rash and most unfortunate man?

OTHELLO

   That's he that was Othello: here I am.

LODOVICO

   Where is that viper? bring the villain forth.

OTHELLO

   I look down towards his feet; but that's a fable.
   If that thou best a devil, I cannot kill thee.

Wounds IAGO

LODOVICO

   Wrench his sword from him.

IAGO

   I bleed, sir; but not kill'd.

OTHELLO

   I am not sorry neither: I'd have thee live;
   For, in my sense, 'tis happiness to die.

LODOVICO

   O thou Othello, thou wert once so good,
   Fall'n in the practice of a damned slave,
   What shall be said to thee?

OTHELLO

   Why, any thing:
   An honourable murderer, if you will;
   For nought I did in hate, but all in honour.

(Act 5, Scene 2)

OR

0 2 *King Lear* – **William Shakespeare**

Read the extract below and answer the question.

Explore the significance of this extract in relation to the tragedy of the play as a whole.

Remember to include in your answer relevant analysis of Shakespeare's dramatic methods.

[25 marks]

ALBANY

   Where have you hid yourself?
   How have you known the miseries of your father?

EDGAR

   By nursing them, my lord. List a brief tale;
   And when 'tis told, O, that my heart would burst!
   The bloody proclamation to escape,
   That follow'd me so near, -O, our lives' sweetness!

That we the pain of death would hourly die
Rather than die at once!- taught me to shift
Into a madman's rags; to assume a semblance
That very dogs disdain'd: and in this habit
Met I my father with his bleeding rings,
Their precious stones new lost: became his guide,
Led him, begg'd for him, saved him from despair;
Never, -O fault!-reveal'd myself unto him,
Until some half-hour past, when I was arm'd:
Not sure, though hoping, of this good success,
I ask'd his blessing, and from first to last
Told him my pilgrimage: but his flaw'd heart,
Alack, too weak the conflict to support!
'Twixt two extremes of passion, joy and grief,
Burst smilingly.

EDMUND

This speech of yours hath moved me,
And shall perchance do good: but speak you on;
You look as you had something more to say.

ALBANY

If there be more, more woeful, hold it in;
For I am almost ready to dissolve,
Hearing of this.

EDGAR

This would have seem'd a period
To such as love not sorrow; but another,
To amplify too much, would make much more,
And top extremity.
Whilst I was big in clamour came there in a man,
Who, having seen me in my worst estate,
Shunn'd my abhorr'd society; but then, finding
Who 'twas that so endured, with his strong arms
He fastened on my neck, and bellow'd out
As he'd burst heaven; threw him on my father;
Told the most piteous tale of Lear and him
That ever ear received: which in recounting
His grief grew puissant and the strings of life
Began to crack: twice then the trumpets sounded,
And there I left him tranced.

ALBANY

But who was this?

EDGAR

Kent, sir, the banish'd Kent; who in disguise
Follow'd his enemy king, and did him service
Improper for a slave.
Enter a Gentleman, with a bloody knife

Gentleman

Help, help, O, help!

EDGAR

What kind of help?

ALBANY

Speak, man.

EDGAR

What means that bloody knife?

Gentleman

'Tis hot, it smokes;
It came even from the heart of-O, she's dead!

ALBANY

Who dead? speak, man.

Gentleman

Your lady, sir, your lady: and her sister
By her is poisoned; she hath confess'd it

(Act 5, Scene 3)

Section B

Answer **one** question in this section.

EITHER

| 0 | 3 | *Othello* – **William Shakespeare**

'Othello's tragedy is caused entirely by his own fatal flaws, and not by the actions of those around him.'

To what extent do you agree with this view?

Remember to include in your answer relevant comment on Shakespeare's dramatic methods.

[25 marks]

OR

| 0 | 4 | *Othello* – **William Shakespeare**

'*Othello* is a tragedy about the dangers of love and betrayal.'

To what extent do you agree with this view?

Remember to include in your answer relevant comment on Shakespeare's dramatic methods.

[25 marks]

OR

| 0 | 5 | *King Lear* – **William Shakespeare**

'*King Lear* is a play which explores the absurdity of power and its division, rather than its destructive nature.'

To what extent do you agree with this view?

Remember to include in your answer relevant comment on Shakespeare's dramatic methods.

[25 marks]

OR

| 0 | 6 | *King Lear* – **William Shakespeare**

'Lear's madness is an illusion, designed to provoke sympathy for his actions.'

To what extent do you agree with this view?

Remember to include in your answer relevant comment on Shakespeare's dramatic methods.

[25 marks]

Section C

Answer **one** question in this section.

In this section you must write about **two** texts. **One** text must be a drama text.

One text must be written pre-1900. You can write about the following texts:

Richard II (pre-1900 drama)
Death of a Salesman (drama)
Tess of the D'Urbervilles (pre-1900)
The Great Gatsby
Keats Poetry Selection (pre-1900)
Poetry Anthology: Tragedy (at least **two** poems must be covered).

EITHER

| 0 | 7 | 'Tragic protagonists are always untrustworthy and unable to fulfil readers' and audiences' expectations.'

To what extent do you agree with this view in relation to **two** texts you have studied?

Remember to include in your answer relevant comment on the ways the writers have shaped meanings.

[25 marks]

OR

| 0 | 8 | 'At the centre of any tragic story lies a sense of sin and guilt.'

To what extent do you agree with this view in relation to **two** texts you have studied?

Remember to include in your answer relevant comment on the ways the writers have shaped meanings.

[25 marks]

Practice Exam 2

A-Level
ENGLISH LITERATURE B

Paper 1B: Literary Genres: Aspects of Comedy

Time allowed: 2 hours 30 minutes

Instructions

- Use black ink or black ball point pen.
- There are three sections: A, B and C.
- Answer **one** question from Section A, **one** from Section B and **one** from Section C.
- You may answer on the same Shakespeare play in Sections A and B.
- For Section C, you must write about **two** texts: **one** pre-1900 drama text and **one** further text
- Write down all of rough work. Cross through any work that you do not want to be marked.

Information

- The maximum mark for this paper is 75.
- The marks for questions are shown in brackets.
- There are 25 marks for Question 1, 25 marks for Question 2 and 25 marks for Question 3

- You will be marked on your ability to:
  - use good English
  - organise information clearly
  - use specialist vocabulary where appropriate.
- In your response you need to:
  - analyse carefully the writers' methods
  - explore the contexts of the texts you are writing about
  - explore connections across the texts you have studied

EITHER

0 1   *The Taming of the Shrew* – **William Shakespeare**

Read the extract below and answer the question.

Explore the significance of this extract in relation to the comedy of the play as a whole.

Remember to include in your answer relevant analysis of Shakespeare's dramatic methods.

[25 marks]

TRANIO
> I pray sir, tell me, is it possible
> That love should of a sudden take such hold?

LUCENTIO
> O Tranio, till I found it to be true
> I never thought it possible or likely.
> But see! While idly I stood looking on,
> I found the effect of love-in-idleness,
> And now in plainness do confess to thee
> That art to me as secret and as dear
> As Anna to the Queen of Carthage was –
> Tranio, I burn! I pine, I perish, Tranio,
> If I achieve not this young modest girl.
> Counsel me, Tranio, for I know thou canst;
> Assist me, Tranio, for I know thou wilt.

TRANIO
> Master, it is no time to chide you now;
> Affection is not rated from the heart.
> If love have touched you, naught remains but so:
> *Redime te captum quam queas minimo.*

LUCENTIO
> Gramercies, lad. Go forward. This contents;
> The rest will comfort, for thy counsel's sound.

TRANIO
> Master, you looked so longly on the maid,
> Perhaps you marked not what's the pith of all.

LUCENTIO
> O yes, I saw sweet beauty in her face,
> Such as the daughter of Agenor had,
> That made great Jove to humble him to her hand
> When with his knees he kissed the Cretan sand.

TRANIO

> Saw you no more? Marked you not how her sister
> Began to scold and raise up such a storm
> That mortal ears might hardly endure the din?

LUCENTIO

> Tranio, I saw her coral lips to move,
> And with her breath she did perfume the air.
> Sacred and sweet was all I saw in her.

TRANIO

> Nay, then, 'tis time to stir him from his trance.
> I pray, awake, sir. If you love the maid
> Bend thoughts and wits to achieve her. Thus it stands:
> Her elder sister is so curst and shrewd
> That, till the father rid his hands of her,
> Master, your love must live a maid at home,
> And therefore has he closely mewed her up,
> Because she will not be annoyed with suitors.

LUCENTIO

> Ah, Tranio, what a cruel father's he!
> But art thou not advised he took some care
> To get her cunning schoolmasters to instruct her?

TRANIO

> Ay, marry I am, sir – and now 'tis plotted!

(Act 1, Scene 1)

OR

0 2 *Twelfth Night* – **William Shakespeare**

Read the extract below and answer the question.

Explore the significance of this extract in relation to the comedy of the play as a whole.

Remember to include in your answer relevant analysis of Shakespeare's dramatic methods.

[25 marks]

VIOLA

> I see what you are. You are too proud;
> But if you were the devil, you are fair!
> My lord and master loves you. O such love
> Could be but recompensed, though you were crowned
> The nonpareil of beauty.

OLIVIA

　　　　　　How does he love me?

VIOLA

With adorations, fertile tears,
With groans that thunder love, with sighs of fire.

OLIVIA

Your lord does know my mind. I cannot love him.
Yet I suppose him virtuous, know him noble,
Of great estate, of fresh and stainless youth;
In voices well divulged, free learned, and valiant,
And in dimension, and the shape of nature,
A gracious person. But yet I cannot love him.
He might have took his answer long ago.

VIOLA

If I did love you, in my master's flame,
With such a suff'ring, such a deadly life,
In your denial I would find no sense;
I would not understand it.

OLIVIA

　　　　　　Why, what would you?

VIOLA

Make me a willow cabin at your gate,
And call upon my soul within the house;
Write loyal cantons of contemned love,
And sing them loud even in the dead of night;
Hallow your name to the reverberate hills.
And make the babbling gossip of the air
Cry out 'Olivia!' O you should not rest
Between the elements of air and earth
But you should pity me!

OLIVIA

　　　　　　You might do much.
What is your parentage?

VIOLA

Above my fortunes, yet my state is well:
I am a gentleman.

OLIVIA

　　　　　　Get you to your lord.
I cannot love him. Let him send no more –
Unless (perchance) you come to me again,
To tell me how he takes it. Fare you well.
I thank you for your pains. Spend this for me.

VIOLA

I am no fee'd post, lady; keep your purse,
My master, not myself, lacks recompense.
Love makes his heart of flint that you shall love,

And let your fervor like my master's be
Placed in contempt. Farewell, fair cruelty.

Exit

OLIVIA

'What is your parentage?'
'Above my fortunes, yet my state is well:
I am a gentleman.' I'll be sworn thou art.
Thy tongue, thy face, thy limbs, actions, and spirit
Do give thee five-fold blazon. Not too fast! Soft, soft!
Unless the master were the man - How now?
Even so quickly may one catch the plague?
Methinks I feel this youth's perfections
With an invisible and subtle stealth
To creep in at mine eyes. Well, let it be.
What ho, Malvolio!

(Act 1, Scene 5)

Section B

Answer **one** question in this section.

EITHER

0	3

The Taming of the Shrew – William Shakespeare

'*The Taming of the Shrew* is a play in praise of marriage.'

To what extent do you agree with this view?

Remember to include in your answer relevant comment on Shakespeare's dramatic methods.

[25 marks]

OR

0	4

The Taming of the Shrew – **William Shakespeare**

'*The Taming of the* Shew is a comedy about transformation.'

To what extent do you agree with this view?

Remember to include in your answer relevant comment on Shakespeare's dramatic methods.

[25 marks]

OR

0	5

Twelfth Night – **William Shakespeare**

'Sir Toby Belch and Sir Andrew Aguecheek's only function is to make the audience laugh.'

To what extent do you agree with this view?

Remember to include in your answer relevant comment on Shakespeare's dramatic methods.

[25 marks]

OR

0	6

Twelfth Night – **William Shakespeare**

'Although *Twelfth Night* follows the conventions of comedy, its mood is dark and at times almost tragic.'

To what extent do you agree with this view?

Remember to include in your answer relevant comment on Shakespeare's dramatic methods.

[25 marks]

Section C

Answer **one** question in this section

In this section you must write about **two** texts, **one** of which must be a pre-1900 drama text.

You can write about the following texts:

She Stoops to Conquer (pre-1900 drama)
The Importance of Being Earnest (pre-1900 drama)
Emma
Small Island
The Nun's Priest's Tale
Poetry Anthology: Comedy

EITHER

0	7

'All good comedies include at least one villain who poses a serious threat and is satisfactorily vanquished.'

To what extent do you agree with this view in relation to **two** texts you have studied?

Remember to include in your answer relevant comment on the ways the writers have shaped meanings.

[25 marks]

OR

0	8

'Differences in social class provide the most fertile ground for writers of comedy.'

To what extent do you agree with this view in relation to **two** texts you have studied?

Remember to include in your answer relevant comment on the ways the writers have shaped meanings.

[25 marks]

Name: ....

Practice Exam 2
A-Level
ENGLISH LITERATURE

Paper 2A: Texts and Genres: Elements of Crime Writing

Time allowed: 3 hours

Materials
For this paper you must have:
- a copy of the set text(s) you have studied for Section B and Section C. These texts must not be annotated and must not contain additional notes or materials.

Instructions
- Use black ink or black ball point pen.
- There are three sections: A, B and C.
- You must answer the question in Section A, **one** question from Section B and **one** question from Section C. Over Section B and Section C, you must write about **three** texts: at least **one** poetry text, **one** post-2000 prose text and **one** further text.

Information
- The maximum mark for this paper is 75.
- The marks for questions are shown in brackets.

- You will be marked on your ability to:
  - use good English
  - organise information clearly
  - use specialist vocabulary where appropriate.
- In your response you need to:
  - analyse carefully the writers' methods
  - explore the contexts of the texts you are writing about
  - explore connections across the texts you have studied
  - Explore different interpretations of your texts

Section A

Answer the question in this section

0 1   Explore the significance of elements of crime writing in this extract. Remember to include in your answer relevant detailed analysis of the ways the author has shaped meanings.

[25 marks]

This extract is taken from Sir Arthur Conan Doyle's short story *The Adventure of the Speckled Band* (published 1893). In it, the narrator Dr Watson tells how Sherlock Holmes solves the murder of Julia Stoner, a case brought to him by the victim's twin sister, Helen. Julia died mysteriously, from no obvious cause, in her locked bedroom at her step-father's house. Now, Helen thinks she too is in danger. Holmes has discovered that there is a very small ventilator, with a bell pull below it, between Helen's (formerly Julia's) room and their stepfather's room. In order to prove Holmes's theory, Holmes and Watson are spending the night in the room.

How shall I ever forget that dreadful vigil? I could not hear a sound, not even the drawing of a breath, and yet I knew that my companion sat open-eyed, within a few feet of me, in the same state of nervous tension in which I was myself. The shutters cut off the least ray of light, and we waited in absolute darkness.

From outside came the occasional cry of a night-bird, and once at our very window a long drawn catlike whine, which told us that the cheetah was indeed at liberty. Far away we could hear the deep tones of the parish clock, which boomed out every quarter of an hour. How long they seemed, those quarters! Twelve struck, and one and two and three, and still we sat waiting silently for whatever might befall.

Suddenly there was the momentary gleam of a light up in the direction of the ventilator, which vanished immediately, but was succeeded by a strong smell of burning oil and heated metal. Someone in the next room had lit a dark-lantern. I heard a gentle sound of movement, and then all was silent once more, though the smell grew stronger. For half an hour I sat with straining ears. Then suddenly another sound became audible—a very gentle, soothing sound, like that of a small jet of steam escaping continually from a kettle. The instant that we heard it, Holmes sprang from the bed, struck a match, and lashed furiously with his cane at the bell-pull.

"You see it, Watson?" he yelled. "You see it?"

But I saw nothing. At the moment when Holmes struck the light I heard a low, clear whistle, but the sudden glare flashing into my weary eyes made it impossible for me to tell what it was at which my friend lashed so savagely. I could, however, see that his face was deadly pale and filled with horror and loathing. He had ceased to strike and was gazing up at the ventilator when suddenly there broke from the silence of the night the most horrible cry to which I have ever listened. It swelled up louder and louder, a hoarse yell of pain and fear and anger all mingled in the one dreadful shriek. They say that away down in the village, and even in the distant parsonage, that cry raised the sleepers from their beds. It struck cold to our hearts, and I stood gazing at Holmes, and he at me, until the last echoes of it had died away into the silence from which it rose.

'What can it mean?' I gasped.

'It means that it is all over,' Holmes answered. 'And perhaps, after all, it is for the best. Take your pistol, and we will enter Dr. Roylott's room.'

With a grave face he lit the lamp and led the way down the corridor. Twice he struck at the chamber door without any reply from within. Then he turned the handle and entered, I at his heels, with the cocked pistol in my hand.

It was a singular sight which met our eyes. On the table stood a dark-lantern with the shutter half open, throwing a brilliant beam of light upon the iron safe, the door of which was ajar. Beside this table, on the wooden chair, sat Dr. Grimesby Roylott clad in a long grey dressing-gown, his bare ankles protruding beneath, and his feet thrust into red heelless Turkish slippers. Across his lap lay the short stock with the long lash which we had noticed during the day. His chin was cocked upward and his eyes were fixed in a dreadful, rigid stare at the corner of the ceiling. Round his brow he had a peculiar yellow band, with brownish speckles, which seemed to be bound tightly round his head. As we entered he made neither sound nor motion.

'The band! the speckled band!' whispered Holmes.

I took a step forward. In an instant his strange headgear began to move, and there reared itself from among his hair the squat diamond-shaped head and puffed neck of a loathsome serpent.

'It is a swamp adder!' cried Holmes; 'the deadliest snake in India. He has died within ten seconds of being bitten. Violence does, in truth, recoil upon the violent, and the schemer falls into the pit which he digs for another. Let us thrust this creature back into its den, and we can then remove Miss Stoner to some place of shelter and let the county police know what has happened.'

As he spoke he drew the dog-whip swiftly from the dead man's lap, and throwing the noose round the reptile's neck he drew it from its horrid perch and, carrying it at arm's length, threw it into the iron safe, which he closed upon it.

Such are the true facts of the death of Dr. Grimesby Roylott, of Stoke Moran. It is not necessary that I should prolong a narrative which has already run to too great a length by telling how we broke the sad news to the terrified girl, how we conveyed her by the morning train to the care of her good aunt at Harrow, of how the slow process of official inquiry came to the conclusion that the doctor met his fate while indiscreetly playing with a dangerous pet. The little which I had yet to learn of the case was told me by Sherlock Holmes as we travelled back next day

Over Section B and Section C, you must write about **three** texts from the following list. At least **one** must be a pre-1900 poetry text. At least **one** must be a post-2000 prose text:

Selected Poems: Crabbe, Browning and Wilde (pre-1900 poetry)
The Rime of the Ancient Mariner (pre-1900 poetry)
Atonement (post-2000 prose)
When Will There Be Good News? (post-2000 prose)
Oliver Twist
The Murder of Roger Ackroyd
Brighton Rock
Hamlet

Section B

Answer **one** question in this section.

EITHER

0 2 *Selected Poems* – GeorgeCrabbe, Robert Browning and Oscar Wilde

'These poets are fascinated by the exercise of power through violence.'

To what extent do you think that the poems in this selection support this view? Remember to include in your answer relevant detailed exploration of the poets' authorial methods.

You should refer to the work of at least **two authors** in your answer.

[25 marks]

OR

0 3 *The Rime of the Ancient Mariner* – Samuel Taylor Coleridge

'The only real victim of the ancient mariner's crime is the ancient mariner himself.'

To what extent do you agree with this view? Remember to include in your answer relevant detailed exploration of Coleridge's authorial methods.

[25 marks]

OR

0 4 *When Will There Be Good News?* – Kate Atkinson

'*When Will There be Good News*? is about revenge, not justice.'

To what extent do you agree with this view? Remember to include in your answer relevant detailed exploration of Atkinson's authorial methods.

[25 marks]

OR

☐0☐5 ***Atonement* – Ian McEwan**

'The real victims of Paul Marshall's crime are Robbie and Cecilia, not Lola and certainly not Briony.'

To what extent do you agree with this view? Remember to include in your answer relevant detailed exploration of McEwan's authorial methods.

[25 marks]

OR

☐0☐6 ***Oliver Twist* – Charles Dickens**

'Bumble says ''the Law is a ass''. Dickens would appear to agree with him as the legal institutions of 19ᵗʰ century Britain are shown in *Oliver Twist* to be completely ineffective.'

To what extent do you agree with this view? Remember to include in your answer relevant detailed exploration of Dickens' authorial methods.

[25 marks]

OR

☐0☐7 ***Brighton Rock* – Graham Greene**

'In *Brighton Rock* Greene distinguishes between Ida's ideas about 'right and wrong' and Pinkie and Rose's sense of 'good and evil' but in practice they are the same.'

To what extent do you agree with this view? Remember to include in your answer relevant detailed exploration of Greene's authorial methods.

[25 marks]

OR

☐0☐8 ***The Murder of Roger Ackroyd* – Agatha Christie**

'Agatha Christie's characters exist in an unreal world where murder causes no grief or pain but is just a puzzle to be solved.'

To what extent do you agree with this view of the novel? Remember to include in your answer relevant detailed exploration of Christie's authorial methods.

[25 marks]

OR

☐0☐9 ***Hamlet* – William Shakespeare**

'The crime of Claudius is so great that it corrupts the court and makes the whole of Denmark 'rotten'.'

To what extent do you agree with this view of *Hamlet*? Remember to include in your answer relevant detailed exploration of Shakespeare's dramatic methods.

[25 marks]

Section C

Answer **one** question in this section.

In your answer you must write about **two** texts that you have **not** used in **Section B**.

EITHER

1 0   'In crime writing the restoration of order and 'normal' life is more important than truth and justice.'

Explore the significance of the restoration of 'normal life' in **two** of the texts you have studied.

[25 marks]

OR

1 1   'Punishment is an essential ingredient of crime literature.'

Explore the significance of punishment in **two** crime texts you have studied.

[25 marks]

Practice Exam 2

A-Level
ENGLISH LITERATURE B

Paper 2B: Texts and Genres: Elements of Political and Social Protest Writing

Time allowed: 3 hours

Materials

For this paper you must have:

- a copy of the set text(s) you have studied for Section B and Section C. These texts must not be annotated and must not contain additional notes or materials.

Instructions

- Use black ink or black ball point pen.
- There are three sections: A, B and C.
- You must answer the question in Section A, **one** question from Section B and **one** question from Section C. Over Section B and Section C, you must write about **three** texts: **one** poetry text, **one** post-2000 prose text and **one** further text. **One** of your texts must be written pre-1900.

Information

- The maximum mark for this paper is 75.
- The marks for questions are shown in brackets.

- You will be marked on your ability to:
  - use good English
  - organise information clearly
  - use specialist vocabulary where appropriate.
- In your response you need to:
  - analyse carefully the writers' methods
  - explore the contexts of the texts you are writing about
  - explore connections across the texts you have studied
  - Explore different interpretations of your texts

Section A

Answer the question in this section.

---

0 1 Explore the significance of elements of social protest writing in this extract. Remember to include in your answer relevant detailed analysis of the ways the author has shaped meanings.

[25 marks]

This poem was written by William Wordsworth in 1804. In it he recreates his feelings (and those of many others) when he heard about the French Revolution (1789–1799). By the time this poem was written, the revolution had turned from its ideals of liberty, equality and fraternity, descending into violence and oppression. Romantic poets like Wordsworth, who had been enthusiastic supporters of the Revolution, were disappointed and disillusioned.

The French Revolution as It Appeared to Enthusiasts at Its Commencement

Oh! pleasant exercise of hope and joy!
For mighty were the auxiliars which then stood
Upon our side, we who were strong in love!
Bliss was it in that dawn to be alive,
But to be young was very heaven!—Oh! times,
In which the meagre, stale, forbidding ways
Of custom, law, and statute, took at once
The attraction of a country in romance!
When Reason seemed the most to assert her rights,
When most intent on making of herself
A prime Enchantress—to assist the work
Which then was going forward in her name!
Not favoured spots alone, but the whole earth,
The beauty wore of promise, that which sets
(As at some moment might not be unfelt
Among the bowers of paradise itself)
The budding rose above the rose full blown.
What temper at the prospect did not wake
To happiness unthought of? The inert
Were roused, and lively natures rapt away!
They who had fed their childhood upon dreams,
The playfellows of fancy, who had made
All powers of swiftness, subtilty, and strength
Their ministers,—who in lordly wise had stirred
Among the grandest objects of the sense,
And dealt with whatsoever they found there
As if they had within some lurking right
To wield it;—they, too, who, of gentle mood,
Had watched all gentle motions, and to these
Had fitted their own thoughts, schemers more wild,
And in the region of their peaceful selves;—
Now was it that both found, the meek and lofty

Did both find, helpers to their heart's desire,
And stuff at hand, plastic as they could wish;
Were called upon to exercise their skill,
Not in Utopia, subterranean fields,
Or some secreted island, Heaven knows where!
But in the very world, which is the world
Of all of us,—the place where in the end,
We find our happiness, or not at all!

(William Wordsworth 1804)

Over **Section B** and **Section C**, you must write about **three** texts from the following list:

Songs of Innocence and of Experience (pre-1900)
Tony Harrison: *Selected Poems*
Harvest (post-2000 prose)
The Kite Runner (post-2000 prose)
A Doll's House (pre-1900)
Hard Times (pre-1900)
Henry IV Part 1 (pre-1900)
The Handmaid's Tale.

Choose **one** of the following combinations:

Songs of Innocence and Experience plus 1 post-2000 prose text plus 1 other text.

Tony Harrison: *Selected Poems* plus 1 post-2000 prose text plus 1 pre-1900 text.

Section B

Answer **one** question in this section

EITHER

| 0 | 2 | *Songs of Innocence and Experience* – **William Blake**

'Blake sees manmade institutions and rules as the enemies of the divine spirit.'

To what extent do you think that the poems in this selection support this view? Remember to include in your answer relevant detailed exploration of Blake's authorial methods.

[25 marks]

OR

| 0 | 3 | *Selected Poems* – **Tony Harrison**

'The problem with Harrison's poetry is that he can never truly speak to or on behalf of the disenfranchised who are the subject of much of his work.'

To what extent do you think that the poems in this selection support this view? Remember to include in your answer relevant detailed exploration of Harrison's authorial methods.

[25 marks]

OR

| 0 | 4 | *The Kite Runner* – **Kahled Hosseini**

'Hosseini's novel provides a sobering account of what revolution can lead to, leaving the reader with the impression that life before change was almost idyllic in comparison.'

To what extent do you agree with this view? Remember to include in your answer relevant detailed exploration of Hosseini's authorial methods.

[25 marks]

OR

☐0☐5 *Harvest* – Jim Crace

'*Harvest* paints a bleak and essentially pessimistic picture of a society where neither the status quo nor change is desirable.'

To what extent do you agree with this view? Remember to include in your answer relevant detailed exploration of Crace's authorial methods.

[25 marks]

OR

☐0☐6 *Hard Times* – Charles Dickens

'In *Hard Times* Dickens presents a version of working class life which is simplistic and sentimental.'

To what extent do you agree with this view? Remember to include in your answer relevant detailed exploration of Dickens' authorial methods.

[25 marks]

OR

☐0☐7 *Henry IV Part 1* – William Shakespeare

'In *Henry IV Part 1* Shakespeare presents rebellion as attractive and exciting.'

To what extent do you agree with this view? Remember to include in your answer relevant detailed exploration of Shakespeare's authorial methods.

[25 marks]

OR

☐0☐8 *A Doll's House* – Henrik Ibsen (Translated by Michael Meyer)

'Nora's rebellion is the selfish act of a spoilt middle-class woman.'

To what extent do you agree with this view of the play? Remember to include in your answer relevant detailed exploration of Ibsen's authorial methods.

[25 marks]

OR

☐0☐9 *The Handmaid's Tale* – Margaret Atwood

'The Handmaid's Tale is not primarily a feminist novel.'

To what extent do you agree with this view? Remember to include in your answer relevant detailed exploration of Atwood's authorial methods.

[25 marks]

Section C

Answer **one** question in this section.

In your answer you must write about **two** texts that you have **not** used in **Section B**.

___

EITHER

| 1 | 0 | 'In literature protest and rebellion always end in failure.'

Explore the significance of the failure of protest and rebellion as presented in **two** political and social protest texts you have studied.

[25 marks]

OR

| 1 | 1 | 'Writers who write about political and social issues are much better at presenting problems than suggesting solutions.'

Explore the significance of giving (or not giving) solutions to problems as it is in **two** political and social protest novels you have studied.

[25 marks]

ANSWERS

Practice Exam 1

A-level English Literature B

Mark scheme

The mark scheme below (out of 25) applies to all questions in both A-level papers that you will take (Paper 1A or Paper 1B **and** Paper 2A or Paper 2B).

Please note that the 5 bands given do not relate directly to A-level grades. It is impossible to give exact equivalents between levels and grades, as the grades are not decided by the Examination Board until all papers have been marked. However, if you want to attain an A or A* you should clearly aim for Band 5, while a mark in Band 1 or 2 will probably be the equivalent of a fail.

There are 5 Assessment Objectives (AOs) referred to in the mark scheme. These are not marked separately and can overlap.

AO1: Articulate informed, personal and creative responses to literary texts, using associated concepts and terminology, and coherent, accurate written expression.

AO2: Analyse ways in which meanings are shaped in literary texts.

AO3: Demonstrate understanding of the significance and influence of the contexts in which literary texts are written and received.

AO4: Explore connections across literary texts.

AO5: Explore literary texts informed by different interpretations

After the mark scheme are examples of the content you might include in your answers.

Band	Typical Features
Band 5 **Perceptive and assured** **21–25** At the top of the band you will have shown yourself to be assured, sensitive and perceptive across all five AOs. At the bottom of the band your answers will be coherent and accurate with some perception.	• AO1 You have made a perceptive, assured and sophisticated argument, focussed on the task. • AO1 You have expressed yourself in a mature and impressive way, using relevant literary and critical concepts and terminology. • AO2 You have shown perceptive understanding of the author's methods. • AO2 You have shown assured engagement with how meanings are shaped by these methods. • AO3 You have shown perceptive understanding of the significance of relevant contexts. • AO3 You have connected those contexts to the genre studied in an assured way. • AO4 You have perceptively explored connections across literary texts arising out of generic study. • AO5 You have engaged perceptively and confidently with the debate set up in the task.
Band 4 **Coherent and thorough** **16–20** At the top of the band you will have made a thorough and coherent argument across all five AOs. At the bottom of the band your ideas will be shaped, relevant and clear with one or two lapses in coherence and accuracy.	• AO1 You have made a logical, thorough and coherent argument, focussed on the task. • AO1 You have expressed yourself precisely and accurately, using appropriate literary and critical concepts and terminology. • AO2 You have shown thorough understanding of the author's methods. • AO2 You have shown thorough engagement with how meanings are shaped by these methods. • AO3 You have shown thorough understanding of the significance of relevant contexts. • AO3 You have connected those contexts to the genre studied in a coherent way. • AO4 You have logically and consistently explored connections across literary texts arising out of generic study. • AO5 You have engaged thoroughly with the debate set up in the task.

Band 3 **Straightforward and relevant** **11–15** At the top of the band you will have shown consistent straightforward understanding, with ideas developed relevantly. At the bottom of the band there will be some relevant understanding and evidence of straightforward thinking.	• AO1 You have ordered ideas sensibly in a relevant argument in relation to the task. • AO1 You have expressed yourself in a straightforward and clear way, making some use of literary and critical concepts and terminology. • AO2 You have shown straightforward understanding of the author's methods. • AO2 You have shown relevant engagement with how meanings are shaped by these methods. • AO3 You have shown straightforward understanding of the significance of relevant contexts. • AO3 You have made relevant connections between those contexts and the genre studied. • AO4 You have explored connections across literary texts arising out of generic study in a straightforward way. • AO5 You have engaged in a straightforward way with the debate set up in the task.
Band 2 **Simple and generalised** **6–10** At the top of the band you will have shown a basic generalised understanding, with ideas developed in a simple way. At the bottom of the band there will be inconsistency but the beginnings of a simple and generalised understanding.	• AO1 You made a simple argument, which may not be consistent but which does relate to the task. • AO1 You have expressed yourself in a simple way, using generalised literary and critical concepts and terminology. • AO2 You have shown simple understanding of the author's methods. • AO2 You have shown generalised engagement with how meanings are shaped by these methods. • AO3 You have shown simple understanding of the significance of relevant contexts. • AO3 You have made generalised connections between those contexts and the genre studied. • AO4 You have explored connections across literary texts arising out of generic study in a simple way. • AO5 You have made a simple and generalised response with the debate set up in the task.
Band 1 **Largely irrelevant, misunderstood and inaccurate** **1–6** At the top of the band you will have made some unconnected points. Your writing will lack clarity. At the bottom of the band there will be no connection with the task; the writing will be hard to follow and irrelevant.	• You will have made some vague points in relation to the task. • Your writing will be unclear and incorrect. If it is accurate, the content will be irrelevant. • You will have shown little sense of the AOs; little sense of how meanings are shaped; little sense of any connection arising out of generic study; little sense of an argument in relation to the task.
0 marks	You have written nothing or your response has no connection to the text(s) **or** task.

Suggested Content

Suggested content is organised according to AOs 2–5. Some suggestions given might address more than one AO.

Practice Papers Set A

Paper 1A

Literary Genres: Aspects of Tragedy

For **AO1** the examiners are looking for the same things for all questions (1–8):
• quality of argument;
• organisation of ideas;
• use of appropriate concepts and terminology;
• technical accuracy.

AO1: It is important that you show that you can use literary terms correctly and with confidence, but you will not be rewarded for just 'spotting' techniques. You must explain how they are used and their effect on the reader or audience.

01 *Othello*

AO2 Focus might be on:

- the scene's position towards the end of the play before the tragedy reaches a climax;
- the gentle, melancholy tone of the scene before the violence of Act 5;
- use of the song;
- the use of two female characters and the contrast between them;
- Desdemona's consciously poetic language – the imagery of the song and its use of repetition, alliteration and rhyme;
- Emilia's down-to-earth short replies and occasional crudeness.

AO3 Focus might be on:

- the setting in Desdemona's bedroom;
- the position of women in society and ideas about marriage;
- the difference in social status between the two characters;
- the significance of Cyprus, its distance from Venice and civilisation;
- the story of Barbary's song and how it belongs to English folk traditions/society rather than to Venice.

AO4 Focus might be on:

- Desdemona's innocence and how she is a victim of Othello's tragedy;
- whether Desdemona herself can be seen as a tragic heroine.

AO5

You could develop any of the points made above and suggest different meanings arising from them as well as audience reactions, for example:

- how far Desdemona is a victim of gender/ethnic differences and/or a victim of Othello's tragic faults;
- the effectiveness of the introduction of the story of Barbary and the song;
- the role and significance of Emilia in the tragedy.

02 *King Lear*

AO2 Focus might be on:

- the significance of the scene structurally – it could be called the inciting incident;
- the scene's formality and the sense that Lear has rehearsed his formal speeches;
- the corresponding formality of Goneril's and Regan's responses;
- the way in which all three use rhetorical devices, such as hyperbole;
- the contrast of the powerful king we see here with Lear in the rest of the play;
- the importance of Cordelia's asides, showing the audience her thought process;
- the contrast of Cordelia's short lines and unadorned language with the language of her sisters.

AO3 Focus might be on:

- possible visual impact of a formal 'set piece', set in the king's court;
- contrast of this setting with later settings outdoors;
- ideas about kingly authority and the divine right of kings;
- whether, if Lear is anointed by God, he has the right to give up power;
- how the idea of dividing the kingdom – and sowing the seeds of conflict – might look to an Elizabethan audience;
- ideas about women and power – Goneril and Regan are married, but Lear gives power to them in their own right;
- marriage as a political tool, shown in the courting of Cordelia by France and Burgundy;
- fairy tale/folk tale elements with the three sisters and the test;
- the idea of 'Britain', which was becoming current under James VI/I.

AO4 Focus might be on:

- Lear shown as powerful and strong, making his fall more dramatic;
- tragic heroes usually being powerful men;
- how in this scene he sows the seeds of his own downfall and that of Britain;
- his arrogance and egotism in demanding his daughters' answers, leading to his rejection of Cordelia and his tragedy;
- the idea of 'hubris' shown in his attitude here.

AO5

You could develop any of the points made above and suggest different meanings arising from them as well as audience reactions, for example:

- views on Lear's actions and how far those, and his character as shown here, are responsible for his tragedy;
- ideas about kingship and power;
- views on the relationship between the political and the personal, as shown in ideas about marriage and parent/child relationships.

AO1/AO5: Make sure that in your Section A answer you refer to other parts of the play. You can write about the extract and then the rest of the play, but it looks more impressive if your points about the rest of the play arise naturally from your comments on the extract.

03 *Othello*

AO2 Focus might be on:

- Desdemona as a secondary character in terms of the size of her part and her relationship with the eponymous hero, Othello;
- her death seen as part of a build-up to Othello's death and, therefore, not meant to have the same impact;
- whether she is a more sympathetic character than Othello, due to her innocence and the sense that she is a victim;
- her singing of the 'willow' song, invoking sorrow in the audience.

AO3 Focus might be on:

- whether her gender may make her tragedy more or less lamentable.
- her death not being seen as a 'tragedy' in dramatic/literary terms: she is just a victim;
- how modern audiences may see her story as more 'tragic' because of her status as a victim: it cannot be her fault, whereas Othello's tragedy is at least partly his fault.

AO4 Focus might be on:

- how, if she has a 'fatal flaw', it is innocence and naivety;
- how she does not fall from greatness;
- her tragedy being similar to that of Juliet, caused by falling in love and defying convention;
- how, unlike Othello, she is not drawn as a complex, tragic character.

AO5

You might have focussed on some of the following ideas:

For the proposition	Against the proposition
How she is easier to sympathise with than Othello, thus making her death more 'lamentable'.	The meaning and relevance of the words 'profound' and 'lamentable'.
The importance of her gender in creating different reactions to and interpretations of her death.	The secondary nature of her character and her lack of complexity.
The idea that her innocence makes her death more tragic.	How she fails to fit with ideas of what a tragic hero should be.

04 *Othello*

AO2 Focus might be on:

- Iago's soliloquies keeping the audience informed of his deceit and contrasting with his behaviour towards Othello;
- how easily Othello is deceived by the visual 'evidence' of the handkerchief;
- how the play's structure shows the audience Iago's version of things becoming 'reality' for Othello;
- dramatic irony of references to 'honesty' throughout the play.

AO3 Focus might be on:

- association of Iago with the devils of medieval plays;
- Othello's ethnicity – 'blackness' associated with evil, whereas it is the white Iago who is the devil here;
- a lack of trust between Othello and Desdemona being inevitable given their different backgrounds;
- the background of Venice and Cyprus and how shifting the action to Cyprus at a time of war takes the characters out of their normal environment into a strange and unpredictable place.

AO4 Focus might be on:

- Othello's trust in appearances and failure to see reality being due to his innate jealousy;
- Iago, as a villain, engineering Othello's downfall by his lying;
- Othello's peripeteia coming as result of his trust in appearances (the handkerchief).

AO5

You might have focussed on some of the following ideas:

For the proposition	Against the proposition
How Othello is brought down by lies and his trust in what he is shown by Iago.	What is meant by the 'reality' of the situation?
The way in which Iago can deceive most characters, including Cassio, Roderigo, Emilia and Desdemona, as well as Othello.	How the real situations – gender and racial issues, life in Venice and Cyprus – make the tragedy happen, Iago just taking advantage of these situations.
Their inability to see the truth or (in Othello's case) believe the truth.	Othello as a tragic hero and, as such, the cause of his own tragedy.

AO3/AO5: When writing about a play, you must demonstrate that you are aware that it was written to be performed, not read. Refer to 'the audience' or 'audiences', comment on the visual impact of the scene and consider alternative interpretations by directors and actors.

05 *King Lear*

AO2 Focus might be on:

- the role of madness in both the main plot and the Gloucester subplot;
- the plotting of Lear's descent into madness;
- the depiction of 'Poor Tom' and how Edgar's false madness compares/contrasts with Lear;
- the change in Lear's language from the formal authoritative language at the start of the play to the disjointed, seemingly nonsensical language of the 'mad scenes';
- the constant presence of the fool.

AO3 Focus might be on:

- the divine right of kings;
- ideas about madness and its origins, e.g. being possessed by devils, the idea of the holy fool;
- how madness/mental problems might have been treated;
- tension between the pagan setting of the play and the Christian assumptions of its audience;
- differences in how Jacobean and modern audiences might react to a king being 'mad';
- how the change in settings, as Lear becomes (or goes) mad, reflect him returning to nature.

AO4 Focus might be on:

- Lear as a tragic hero – his descent into madness charting his downfall;
- whether his becoming mad represents the peripeteia of his tragedy;
- his madness as a way of finding truth and catharsis;
- ideas about a tragic hero being great/noble and, therefore, his downfall (here to madness) being more to be pitied and wondered at.

AO5

You might have focussed on some of the following ideas:

For the proposition	Against the proposition
The way madness is used to show Lear's tragic downfall.	The fact that when Lear goes mad he is no longer king; when he divides up Britain and rejects Cordelia he does not appear to be mad.
Its prominence as a recurring theme and treatment in different ways (Edgar pretending to be mad; the fool as professional madness).	How it is not madness that is cause of Lear's tragedy but his hubris; madness is the effect.
How a king's descent into madness has an effect on his kingdom; Lear's madness reflecting the chaos of Britain.	Ways in which madness is good for Lear, purging him and bringing him redemption.

06 *King Lear*

AO2 Focus might be on:

- the fool's role as Lear's confidant;
- the difference between the fool's language and that of other characters;
- his use of imagery;
- the crudity/bawdiness of his language;
- the effect of his disappearance before the end of the play;
- his function in releasing tension by providing comic moments.

AO3 Focus might be on:

- the tradition of kings keeping fools;
- ideas about fools having a privileged position at court and being able to tell the truth;
- the fool as a professional entertainer;
- whether the fool is in a sense 'mad';
- fools portrayed as child-like and innocent;
- ideas about the fool and Cordelia being played by the same actor.

AO4 Focus might be on:

- fools being more common in Shakespearean comedy;
- his privileged position allowing him to challenge Lear without repercussions (unlike Kent and Cordelia);
- his challenges to Lear causing Lear to change.

AO5

You might have focussed on some of the following ideas:

For the proposition	Against the proposition
How the fool can speak the truth to Lear and the effect of this.	The meaning of the word 'enlightened' and whether the fool can truly be said to have any special insight.
How his presence allows Shakespeare to explore ideas about madness.	His limited role; how he challenges Lear and supports him but does not do much more.
How he gives the audience an insight into Lear's mind and perhaps helps it to be more sympathetic to Lear.	How other characters (Kent, Edgar, Cordelia) see the truth, and are therefore 'enlightened', and express themselves more clearly and fully than the fool does.

AO1/AO5: Many of the questions in your exams ask 'to what extent' you agree with the statement given. You may agree strongly, disagree strongly or anything in between. Be honest but make sure that, before coming to a conclusion, you consider both sides of the argument.

Section C

For **AO2** the examiners are looking for the same things in both questions 7 and 8. Focus might be on:

- the structure of the drama text in relation to the text;
- the use of dialogue, dramatic action, exits and entrances, soliloquies, flashbacks in the drama text;
- the possible use of a poetry text or a novel and how their methods shape meaning;
- the writers' uses of structural, linguistic and other devices to shape meaning.

07

AO3 Focus might be on:

- ideas about kingship in Richard II, belief in the divine right of kings and concerns about rebellion;
- the idea of the American Dream and materialism in *Death of a Salesman* and *The Great Gatsby*;
- ideas about women and equality in *Tess of the D'Urbervilles*;
- the use of classical myth and legend in 'Tithonus' and 'Lamia';
- the Christian context of *The Monk's Tale*.

AO4 Focus might be on:

- the importance of the idea of catharsis for audiences and readers;
- how the end of a tragedy often feels inevitable, resulting from the characters and actions of the protagonists, e.g. *Tess of the D'Urbervilles*, *Richard II*;
- how readers and audiences can learn from experiencing suffering and sorrow through fiction: *The Monk's Tale* is explicitly didactic; we might draw conclusions about how to behave from the fate of characters such as Tess, Richard II and Gatsby.

AO5

You might have focussed on some of the following ideas:

For the proposition	Against the proposition
How, although Richard II might be sympathetic and at times impressive, the restoration of order by Bolingbroke seems like the right result.	Richard's downfall seen as the result of politics and war and his character as unsympathetic.
Willy Loman's increasing understanding, our awareness of his family's love and a feeling that death might have been the only way out for him.	Willy Loman's death as a pointless waste, possibly leaving the audience feeling depressed.
Tess's death as a kind of triumph or sacrifice.	Tess's death as the result of a cruel fate and the society she lives in.
A feeling that Gatsby has paid for his errors but leaves behind something beautiful and memorable, from which Nick has learned.	Gatsby's tragedy representing the failure of his dreams and leaving readers with a cynical view of a selfish society.
The sense in Keats's poetry that intense love must involve suffering, but love can live on after death.	The fate of the knight in 'La Belle Dame Sans Merci' and Isabella, leaving both the characters and readers unsatisfied. Tithonus's story having no end, as he is condemned to immortality, thereby bringing no sense of catharsis or satisfaction; 'Death in Leamington' and 'Miss Gee' leaving readers with a sense of sadness at the reality of dying alone.

08

AO3 Focus might be on:

- the power of kings such as Richard and Cuchulain and the effects of war;
- the effect of attitudes to marriage and sex in 20th century America (*The Great Gatsby* and *Death of a Salesman*); Gatsby's and Willy's influence on others related to materialism and capitalism;
- Tess's family as victims of society, seen in terms of class, gender and religion;
- *The Monk's Tale* and *Paradise Lost* seen in the context of Christian tradition.

AO4 Focus might be on:

- Richard II and Gatsby having power and wealth; others being dependent on them and drawn into their tragedies; Willy being powerful within his family and his actions causing their tragedies;
- Tess Durbeyfield not seeking to hurt others but causing others suffering, whether physically or mentally; Lorenzo and Isabella's love causing death for one and misery for the other;
- Whether there is always a tragic hero ('Miss Gee'; 'Death in Leamington') and whether it is always clear who is the tragic hero (Isabella or Lorenzo; Lycius or Lamia).

AO5

You might have focussed on some of the following ideas:

For the proposition	Against the proposition
How Richard as king is identified with England and so his tragedy, caused by his own selfish actions, is a tragedy for the whole country; how audiences might feel more sympathy for the Queen.	Richard's unsuitability for the role of king and his enemies' ruthlessness.
Willy's actions being essentially selfish, his unfaithfulness, his attitude to Biff and Happy.	How Willy is an 'everyman' character, eliciting the sympathy of the audience, and is unaware of the effect of his actions on his family.
Tess's tragedy being at least in part the result of her own actions; her family suffers and her child dies; she murders Alec after becoming his lover because Angel Clare has reappeared.	Tess's essential innocence and victimhood, and how Angel and Alec suffer because of their actions towards her.
How the lives of Daisy, Tom, Myrtle and George are all changed by being drawn into Gatsby's worlds and they are, in a sense, his victims.	How Gatsby improves the lives of those around him and it is not he who causes them harm but their own actions (Tom and Myrtle's affair for example).
Cuchulain being responsible for his own son's death; Lucifer and Adam being responsible for bringing sin and misery to the world (making us all the victims of their tragedies).	How the protagonists in Keats's poems tend to be the victims, their tragedies caused by love.

Tithonus being the only victim of his tragedy, as are Miss Gee and the woman in 'Death in Leamington', whose stories have little or no effect on others. |

AO1/AO4: In Section C you are required to write about two texts. Give them equal consideration. You can write about one and then the other, but it is better to compare them as you go, looking at different aspects of the question in relation to both texts.

Paper 1B

Literary Genres: Aspects of Comedy

For **AO1**, the examiners are looking for the same things for all questions (1–8):

- quality of argument;
- organisation of ideas;
- use of appropriate concepts and terminology;
- technical accuracy.

AO1/AO2: It is important that you show that you can use literary terms correctly and with confidence but you will not be rewarded for just 'spotting' techniques. You must explain how they are used and their effect on the reader or audience.

01 *The Taming of the Shrew*

AO2 Focus might be on:

- the significance of the scene structurally – a turning point in the plot;
- the visual impact of the way Petruchio is dressed here;
- the repetition of 'entreat' and 'content' to comic effect in the quickfire exchange at the start of the extract;
- Katherina's use of commands, showing her nature;
- Petruchio's long speech, using rhetorical devices and almost biblical language to impose his authority;
- the nature of the exit and its comic effect. (Does he drag or carry her?)

AO3 Focus might be on:

- Elizabethan ideas of marriage – many upper-class marriages might be arranged by fathers, but audiences might also expect there to be love;
- the widely accepted idea, based on religious teaching, that women should obey their husbands;
- humour caused by Katherina's refusal to bow to this convention;
- how Katherina commands her father – role reversal;
- changes in ideas about marriage and women's role over time and how they might affect audience reactions.

AO4 Focus might be on:

- the marriage happening in the middle of the play rather than at the end, more usual in comedies;
- marriages in comedies usually being love matches; defiance of this convention causing humour here;
- the convention in comedy of the man and woman often fighting and overcoming misunderstandings before falling in love;
- the comments of Baptista, Gremio and Tranio at the end of the extract reflecting audience reaction.

AO5

You could develop any of the points made above and suggest different meanings arising from them as well as audience reactions, for example:

- views on how the scene encapsulates the relationship between Katherina and Petruchio and how it develops;
- views on gender roles, how they are depicted here and how their changing nature affects perceptions of the play;
- consideration of where the comedy comes from (e.g. role reversal, physical comedy) and how it could be effectively conveyed in performance.

02 *Twelfth Night*

AO2 Focus might be on:

- the significance of the scene structurally as the beginning of Toby and Maria's plot against Malvolio;
- the use of broad comedy to contrast with the romantic comedy of the main plot;
- the use of prose;
- contrast between Malvolio's formality and the drunken nonsense of Toby's lines.

AO3 Focus might be on:

- the setting in Olivia's garden and the larger setting of Illyria;
- the traditions of Twelfth Night – drink, celebration and misrule;
- the relative social status of the characters;
- Malvolio as a representation of puritans, their opposition to the theatre and use as figures of fun in drama.

AO4 Focus might be on:

- the use of a subplot, more broadly comic than the main plot;
- humour at the expense of arrogant authority figures;
- the presence of the fool (Feste).

AO5

You could develop any of the points made above and suggest different meanings arising from them as well as audience reactions, for example:

- the contrast between Malvolio and the 'comic' characters, how this reflects Jacobean society and how it will lead to a darker comedy;
- views on the relevance of the title and how this scene reflects the world being turned upside down;
- ideas about the function and significance of the 'comic' characters in the play as a whole.

AO1/AO5: Make sure that in your Section A answer you refer to other parts of the play. You can write about the extract and then the rest of the play, but it looks more impressive if your points about the rest of the play arise naturally from your comments on the extract.

03 *The Taming of the Shrew*

AO2 Focus might be on:

- the structure of the play, following Petruchio's 'taming' of Katherina;
- the impact of the ending when Katherina is subdued;
- the use of language such as 'shrew' to describe Katherina;
- Petruchio's soliloquy and other long speeches;
- the function of Bianca and the widow.

AO3 Focus might be on:

- the inequality in gender roles at the time making it impossible for women to 'win';
- the idea of obedience in marriage;
- modern productions, in keeping with feminist thought, possibly implying a different outcome.

AO4 Focus might be on:

- the play as a comedy and how the outcome, therefore, is not meant to be taken seriously;
- the effect the induction might have on audience perspectives;
- the play as a broad, slapstick comedy, using stereotypes.

AO5

You might have focussed on some of the following ideas:

For the proposition	Against the proposition
The impact of the ending and Katherina's apparent willing acceptance of Petruchio's authority.	Different interpretations of the ending in production.
How the play reflects Elizabethan ideas about marriage and women's roles and, like many comedies, reinforces accepted social norms.	The idea that marriage is shown as a meeting of equals, that Katherina is joining. Petruchio in a 'game' or that she is showing love for him rather than submission.
Katherina's character and how she refuses to conform, but is forced to in the end.	The sudden change in Katherina being unconvincing and/or disturbing.
How Katherina shows the widow and Bianca, and by implication the audience, how they ought to behave and accept men's authority.	How Bianca and widow do not obey their husbands at the end, contrasting with Katherina.

04 *The Taming of the Shrew*

AO2 Focus might be on:

- the separate introductions of Petruchio and Katherina, revealing their faults;
- the premise of the play being the difficulty of finding Katherina a husband;
- Katherina's imperfections vividly shown in her confrontations with Bianca and Hortensio (as Litio);
- Katherina's aggressive language at the beginning of the play and gentle language towards the end;
- Petruchio's interaction with his servant Grumio;
- the visual impact of the kiss in the street.

AO3 Focus might be on:

- arranged marriages/marriage for money not being unusual for upper-class people in the 16th century;
- different attitudes to love and marriage across time;
- the Italian setting, its 'foreignness' emphasised by the induction being in Warwickshire.

AO4 Focus might be on:

- audience expectations of a comedy having a happy ending when the main characters have overcome obstacles to find love;
- much of the comedy being broad, even slapstick, exposing their faults to laughter;
- Elizabethan audience's expectations of order being restored at the end of a play.

AO5

You might have focussed on some of the following ideas:

For the proposition	Against the proposition
How both characters are shown to have faults.	How the focus of the play is on Katherina's faults rather than Petruchio's.
How Petruchio comes to love Katherina despite having married for money.	A sense that he only comes to love her when she submits to him.
Katherina's submission to Petruchio showing love rather than just obedience.	Her submission coming not from love but from abuse.
How their mutual love is demonstrated by the kiss in the street and their subsequent actions.	The unsatisfactory nature of the ending, shown by the many ways in which it has been interpreted.

AO3/AO5: When writing about a play, you must demonstrate that you are aware that it was written to be performed, not read. Refer to 'the audience' or 'audiences', comment on the visual impact of the scene and consider alternative interpretations by directors and actors.

05 *Twelfth Night*

AO2 Focus might be on:

- the subplot of Malvolio's 'madness';
- references to madness (Sebastian speculates Olivia may be mad) as well as to folly and people losing their wits;
- the character of Feste, the fool, who draws attention to the madness of others.

AO3 Focus might be on:

- differing attitudes to madness/mental health in 17th and 21st centuries;
- causes of madness – possession – love as a kind of possession;
- ideas about the humours, especially melancholy, which both Olivia and Orsino suffer from/indulge in;
- the 'madness' associated with Twelfth Night when everything is turned upside down, as it might be by love;
- the setting in the unreal world of Illyria.

AO4 Focus might be on:

- how in comedies characters are changed by love;
- comic plots depending on misunderstandings and people acting strangely;
- the disorder of the play being temporary as the seeming madness of love is, order being restored at the end.

AO5

You might have focussed on some of the following ideas:

For the proposition	Against the proposition
How Malvolio's love for Olivia is used to bring him to madness.	Malvolio's madness being caused by trickery, not his emotions.
How characters are disturbed by their emotions and act out of character.	The characters feelings not being entirely natural but sometimes misplaced for the purposes of the plot.
Confusion akin to madness caused by disguise and mistaken identity.	How confusion caused by disguise and mistaken identity places obstacles in the way of true love and for the audience are part of the fun of *Twelfth Night*.
Ideas about sense and truth being found in madness just as fools are often wise.	How love is seen ultimately as creating stability and order in the world.

06 *Twelfth Night*

AO2 Focus might be on:

- disguise used to drive the plot;
- dramatic irony created by the audience's awareness of Viola's identity;
- the striking visual images of Viola first appearing as a boy and later meeting her reflection in Sebastian;
- the impact of Malvolio's appearance in cross garters;
- the comedy and pathos created by Feste's disguise as Sir Topas.

AO3 Focus might be on:

- possible extra layer of humour created in Jacobean theatre by boys playing female parts;
- difference in gender roles making Viola's disguise liberating;
- different attitudes within audiences to cross dressing/gender confusion;
- dressing up as part of traditional Christmas celebrations.

AO4 Focus might be on:

- how in comedies disguise often enables characters to express themselves more freely and find love;
- confusion created by disguise creates physical comedy, as in the duel;
- comedy created for the audience by characters being fooled.

AO5

You might have focussed on some of the following ideas:

For the proposition	Against the proposition
Ideas about Viola's disguise being liberating and empowering.	The problems and grief caused by Viola's disguise for herself and others.
How her disguise, despite causing problems, in the end helps her and others to find love.	How easily the play could have ended in heartbreak if Sebastian had not turned up.
The almost mystical way in which Viola 'becomes' her twin, yet Sebastian is incomplete as a person until they are reunited.	The sense of her incompleteness and her grief emphasised by her disguise.
The disguised Feste teaching Malvolio a lesson and defeating the forces of Puritanism.	The cruelty of Feste's use of disguise to trick Malvolio and the effect of his trick on the ending of the play.

AO1/AO5: Many of the question in your exams ask 'to what extent' you agree with the statement given. You may agree strongly, disagree strongly or anything in between. Be honest but make sure that, before coming to a conclusion, you consider both sides of the argument.

Section C

For **AO2** the examiners are looking for the same focus in both questions 7 and 8:

- the structure of the drama text in relation to the text;
- the use of dialogue, dramatic action, exits and entrances, and soliloquies in the drama text;
- the possible use of a poetry text or a novel and how their methods shape meaning;
- the writers' uses of structural, linguistic and other devices to shape meaning.

07

AO3 Focus might be on:

- the class-based nature of society shown in *She Stoops to Conquer* and *Emma*;
- racial and class tensions in *Small Island*;

- *The Nun's Priest's Tale* seen in the context of Christian tradition;
- gender differences and relationships between men and women in *Emma*, *Small Island*, *She Stoops to Conquer*, *The Importance of Being Earnest* and anthology poems;
- the inversion of the traditional elegy in 'A Satirical Elegy'.

AO4 Focus might be on:

- *She Stoops to Conquer* and *The Importance of Being Earnest* seen as 'comedies of manners', involving wit which can seem cruel;
- physical violence in the *Nun's Priest's Tale*, 'Sunny Prestatyn' and *Small Island*;
- satire used to mock powerful or pretentious in 'A Satirical Elegy' and *Emma*.

AO5

You might have focussed on some of the following ideas:

For the proposition	Against the proposition
The way Goldsmith encourages the audience to laugh at Mrs Hardcastle and Tony.	The good-natured tone of the humour in *She Stoops to Conquer* and the fact that Tony confronts Hastings about his attitude and receives an apology.
Laughter at the expense of the harmless Miss Prism in *The Importance of Being Earnest*.	The generally warm attitude to Miss Prism, especially from Cecily, and the fact that everything turns out well for all the characters in *The Importance of Being Earnest*.
Emma's snobbish attitude to Miss Bates and, to some extent to the pretentious Mrs Elton, and humour at the expense of elderly Mr Woodhouse.	Mr Knightley's correction of Emma's behaviour; her care for Mr Woodhouse and others.
How Hortense's naivety, as well as her pretensions, are exposed to ridicule and how Bernard is made a fool of in *Small Island*.	The gentle tone of the humour at Hortense's expense and the context of her growth; a feeling that Bernard deserves what he gets because of his racism.
The savage killing of Pertelote and the idea that the priest may be mocking the Prioress in *The Nun's Priest's Tale*.	Pertelote's death not being intended to invoke laughter; mockery of the Prioress being implied and deserved.
The violence done to the poster girl in 'Sunny Prestatyn'; the implied mockery of the mother in 'My Rival's House'; the open mockery of Sisyphus in 'Mrs Sisyphus'; the mockery of a dead man in 'A Satirical Elegy on the Death of a Late Famous General'.	The humour of many of the anthology poems, such as 'Sunny Prestatyn', being observational with no intention of cruelty; the warmth and humanity of poems such as 'Tam O'Shanter' and 'Not My Best Side'.

08

AO3 Focus might be on:

- a general acceptance of how society is structured reflected in the upper/middle-class worlds of *She Stoops to Conquer*, *Emma* and *The Importance of Being Earnest*;
- Christian ideas about salvation reflected in *The Nun's Priest's Tale*;
- humour provided by the re-imagining of old stories in 'Not My Best Side' and 'Mrs Sisyphus'.

AO4 Focus might be on:

- the tradition of comedies ending in marriages and happiness after obstacles have been overcome, seen in *The Importance Being Earnest*, *She Stoops to Conquer* and *Emma*;
- misunderstandings causing confusion and humour in *The Importance of Being Earnest* and *She Stoops to Conquer*;
- characters learning from their mistakes and putting things right in *Emma*, *She Stoops to Conquer*, *The Nun's Priest's Tale* and *Small Island*;

AO5

You might have focussed on some of the following ideas:

For the proposition	Against the proposition
The marriages at the end of *She Stoops to Conquer* giving a happy ending based on true love, but also seeming 'right' in terms of social class and stability.	The unreality of the world of *The Importance of Being Earnest*, the ending being a fantasy of happiness.
How characters are paired off happily, after overcoming misunderstandings and prejudices, in *The Importance of Being Earnest*.	Emma's world and that of the other characters having changed as they have learned the truth about themselves and others.
How Emma's marriage is a love match but is also suitable in social and financial terms, and how Harriet also finds love with a man from a suitable background.	The end of *Small Island* as the beginning of Hortense's life in England, society's problems not having gone away.
Small Island ending on a hopeful note when Hortense takes Queenie's baby.	Chanticleer only just managing to get away; Pertelote's death and his new awareness of the danger posed by the fox.

In *The Nun's Priest's Tale*, how Chanticleer saves himself from the fox and returns to his old life.	How in 'Tam O'Shanter' the devil does not cease to exist because Tam escapes; how 'My Rival's House', 'Sunny Prestatyn' and 'Mrs Sisyphus' do not end with the world returning to normal.
Tam O'Shanter's excessive drinking leading to his encounter with the devil and Nannie; how he learns his lesson and returns to his wife.	

AO1/AO4: In Section C you are required to write about two texts. Give them equal consideration. You can write about one and then the other, but it is better to compare them as you go, looking at different aspects of the question in relation to both texts.

Paper 2A

Texts and Genres: Elements of Crime Writing

For **AO1** the examiners are looking for the same things for all questions (1–11):

- quality of argument;
- organisation of ideas;
- use of appropriate concepts and terminology;
- technical accuracy.

Make sure that every point you make is rooted firmly in the text, avoiding speculation and generalisation. Use plenty of short, embedded quotations to illustrate your points.

Section A

01

AO2 Focus might be on:

- omniscient narrator;
- free indirect discourse ('It mustn't happen');
- change in focus from Dick to Perry near the end;
- flashback, indicated by use of the past perfect ('had');
- brief flash forward in parentheses;
- use of dialogue;
- short sentences (simple sentences, minor sentences) in dialogue;
- descriptive detail ('jelly beans' etc.);
- colloquial language in speech marks;
- rhetorical questions;
- irony ('Here to hunt?');
- creation of tension.

AO3 Focus might be on:

- setting in gas station;
- context of time – murders have been committed;
- American setting established with slang and references to place;
- similarity to American 'road trip' fiction;
- ideas about criminal psychology;
- sense of a violent society.

AO4 Focus might be on:

- basis in a real crime: readers may know the outcome, decreasing tension;
- point of view of the criminals;
- exploration of the aftermath of the murders;
- no sense of guilt or consideration for the victims;
- psychology of the killers;
- James Spor as witness;
- implications of 'non-fiction novel' or 'faction' genre – how much is fact and how much fiction?

AO5

You may have developed any of the above points, suggesting what meanings arise from them and how readers might react, for example:

- sense of how the killers' minds work and how they have reacted to the killing (contrast between them);
- effect on readers of the awareness that this really happened, for example: a lack of tension about ultimate outcome; interest in 'why' rather than 'who' did it;
- sense of Dick's attitude to crime: professional, cool and detached.

Section B

Before you choose which text to answer on, think carefully about not only the questions in Section B on the texts you have studied but also the general questions in Section C and which texts give you the most scope for answering those questions.

02 *Selected Poems* – George Crabbe, Robert Browning and Oscar Wilde

AO2 Focus might be on:

- beginnings and endings;
- use of climaxes;
- use of rhyme and rhythm;
- use of narrative verse paragraphs in 'Peter Grimes';
- dramatic monologue form in Browning;
- ballad form in Wilde;
- use of voices (personae in Browning) and narrative viewpoint;
- language and linguistic devices (patterning, imagery etc.).

AO3 Focus might be on:

- use of settings;
- readers' fascination with the criminal mind;
- the effect of religion on Peter Grimes;
- Browning's interest in psychology and extreme behaviour;
- Wilde's interest in the experience of punishment rather than crime;
- Crabbe's moralistic and didactic interpretation of his subject.

AO4 Focus might be on:

- interest in the criminal's motivation and state of mind;
- how the narrators reveal the criminals' psychology;
- what we learn of the criminal's motivation and background;
- the lack of a voice given to the victims;
- whether and how the criminal is punished.

AO5

You might have focussed on some of the following ideas:

For the proposition	Against the proposition
Browning's use of dramatic monologues to give us insight into criminal minds, showing everything from their point of view and not allowing us access to the victims' feelings.	Sympathy for Browning's victims based on their innocence and beauty (Porpyhria; the Duchess) or the suffering inflicted on them or planned for them.
Peter Grimes's background and motivation, and the emphasis on his conscience and fear of damnation, while his victims are mostly nameless and their feelings are not explored.	Horror and moral revulsion that readers might feel at Peter's crimes, and the youth and innocence of the boys he murders.
Wilde's empathy for the condemned man, partly arising from his own status as a criminal/prisoner, and the lack of references to victims.	Wilde's concern being more about the wider issues of crime and punishment than about individuals.

03 *The Rime of the Ancient Mariner*

AO2 Focus might be on:

- the narrative frame;
- beginning and ending;
- the seven parts of the narrative;
- use of climaxes;
- use of rhyme and rhythm;
- use of voices;
- language of crime and punishment;
- linguistic devices;
- patterning;
- religious imagery.

AO3 Focus might be on:

- the use of settings;
- ideas about exploration/discovery and 'playing God';
- religious context – the albatross as Christ;
- romantic ideas about man and nature.

AO4 Focus might be on:

- the mariner 'confesses' his crime to the wedding guest;
- his punishment and its effect on him;
- his killing of the albatross as a crime against God and/or nature;
- the other sailors as victims of his crime;
- the act seen as sin rather than crime and the distinction to be made.

AO5

You might have focussed on some of the following ideas:

For the proposition	Against the proposition
The violence of the act and how the albatross is seen as a 'Christian soul' or even Christ, which would make the action a serious crime.	Definitions of 'crime' – perhaps taking a wider view of what the word means (more like a sin).
The fact that the albatross is a bird and that it is (or certainly was) not a crime to kill a bird.	The existence of other (human) victims of the mariner's action, suggesting the mariner has committed a crime.
The mariner's feelings of guilt and his punishment.	His punishment not being the result of any judicial process.
Suspense about the outcome for the mariner and the crew.	The lack of a sense of mystery about either who committed the 'crime' or why he committed it.

AO2/AO4: You need to demonstrate your understanding of poetic techniques, forms and movements but you must write about these in terms of the poetry as writing about crime, for example: how does the use of the dramatic monologue affect your response to the crime?

04 *When Will There Be Good News?*

AO2 Focus might be on:

- beginning and ending;
- use of climaxes relating to emotions;
- use of interconnected stories;
- omniscient narrator and free indirect discourse;
- use of dialogue;
- linguistic devices;
- literary allusions;
- use of humour;
- cyclical structure.

AO3 Focus might be on:

- use of settings;
- focus on victims of crime and their reactions;
- 21st century ideas about marriage/sexual fidelity;
- gender issues and feminist slant of novel;
- families centred on mother/child relationships with fathers absent or useless;
- relative morality, driven by emotion rather than fixed ideas of right and wrong.

AO4 Focus might be on:

- interplay between professional and private lives of Brodie and Munroe;
- love as a motivation for killing;
- love blinding characters to faults of others and resulting in their involvement in crimes.

AO5

You might have focussed on some of the following ideas:

For the proposition	Against the proposition
Jo's mother saving her at the beginning and her survival being the catalyst for the rest of the novel.	Jo's mother's failure to protect the rest of the family; her father's lack of love for them causing them to be there.
Jo's love for her child motivating her to kill her kidnappers.	How far her actions are motivated by love and how far by revenge and the psychological effects of her past.
Her love for her husband causing her to be unwittingly involved in his crimes, resulting in her being kidnapped.	The unsatisfactory relationships between the Turners and whether they do love each other.
The recurring theme of mothers' love or lack of love for their children and how it has shaped them.	The fact that none of the mothers are still alive and able to give love; characters being damaged by lack of love from either parent.

Brodie's love for his dead sister providing motivation for him as a detective.	Brodie's and Munroe's actions having little or nothing to do with love.
His love for 'Tessa' causing him to become a victim for crime.	Brodie's marriage showing his weakness.
Brodie and Munroe's mutual attraction.	Lack of sympathy felt by some readers for any of the characters, who seem cold and unable to love.

05 Atonement

AO2 Focus might be on:

- beginning and ending;
- use of climaxes;
- use of different timelines, related to each other;
- the postmodern ending, drawing attention to it being fiction;
- use of the (apparently) third-person narrator;
- the unreliability of the narrator in hindsight;
- use of irony;
- significance of the title.

AO3 Focus might be on:

- the setting in an upper-class country house;
- issues of social class and the behaviour of upper-class families;
- sexual morality at the time when it is set and the time when it was written;
- gender roles across time;
- Briony's age and whether she is considered legally responsible.

AO4 Focus might be on:

- the setting recalling country house mysteries of the 1920s and '30s;
- subversion of the norms of the crime novel, as criminals are rewarded rather than punished, while an innocent man is punished;
- Briony's guilty conscience and how she deals with it by fictionalising the events;
- her punishment of herself and trying to make up for her crime by doing good through nursing.

AO5

You might have focussed on some of the following ideas:

For the proposition	Against the proposition
The title of the novel and the idea that, by writing it, she has atoned for her past.	The way Briony's emergence as an unreliable narrator makes the reader doubt everything that has gone before and see her novel as an exercise in self-justification or even a deception of the reader.
The emphasis throughout on her feelings of guilt and how she has been unable to put things right.	Awareness that, after the crime, she had opportunities to confess and a feeling that her reasons for not doing so are unconvincing and that (unlike in the 'fictional' ending) she does not put things right with Cecelia and Robbie.
Sympathy for her from readers (and author) because of her age and her emotions at the time of her false accusation.	A sense that, as an intelligent 13-year-old, she is old enough to take responsibility for her actions; a feeling that her class, age and gender have combined to put her above the law.
Her crime being less serious than that of Paul Marshall, who escapes unpunished.	Her being an accessory to Paul Marshall's crime and the sense that they have both been rewarded for wrongdoing, while Cecelia and Robbie have had their happiness brutally cut short.

AO3/AO5: Context includes the context of how texts are received. Beware of assuming that all 21st century readers will bring the same ideas and assumptions and react in the same way. Look up reviews on the internet and talk to other people who have read the books to stimulate thought and provide different perspectives.

06 Oliver Twist

AO2 Focus might be on:

- the picaresque structure;
- the conventional ending, the criminals being punished;
- the use of fiction to expose social problems;
- the third-person intrusive narrator;
- the narrator's explorations of the minds of Nancy and Sykes;
- the use of 'cant' (thieves' slang) in the criminals' dialogue;
- the violent language of Sykes;
- the vivid descriptions of violence.

AO3 Focus might be on:

- the setting in 1830s London, emphasising poverty and squalor;
- contrast with settings in the country and at Mr Brownlow's house;
- The Poor Law Act of 1834 and the harshness of the workhouses;
- the constant threat of severe punishment – hanging or transportation;
- Dickens's attitude to the institutions of the law as incompetent and/or corrupt;
- Dickens's take on gender differences leading to sympathy for Nancy;
- Differences between 19th and 21st century attitudes to crimes, for example: modern readers might take a harsher view of Fagin 'grooming' children.

AO4 focus might be on:

- the London settings creating a sense of danger and evil;
- scenes in court, showing how justice is or is not served (sometimes treated comically);
- the inadequacy of law enforcement and how justice is only done because of middle-class amateurs seeking the truth;
- an interest in feelings of guilt and its effect on the criminals;
- the tying up of loose ends when punishment and rewards are meted out at the end;
- the variety of criminal acts depicted, climaxing in murder.

AO5

You might have focussed on some of the following ideas:

For the proposition	Against the proposition
The strong sense that the criminals are trapped in their life by poverty and lack of opportunity.	The awareness that there are other poor characters who are not criminals; Oliver's ability to resist doing wrong; and Charley's eventual reformation.
The entertaining and often humorous portrayal of Fagin's gang (Oliver's training; the descriptions of the boys; the chase through the streets). Awareness that the gang are very young (paradoxically innocent).	How, as the novel progresses, the dark side of their criminality is shown with the emphasis shifting to Monks's plot and Sykes's violence, as well as their willingness to betray each other.
Fagin portrayed at times as almost paternalistic, seeming to care for the gang; modern sympathies for him as an outsider in society.	Fagin's true nature, revealed in his involvement with Monks.
Sympathy induced by the severity of the punishments for their crimes.	A feeling that most of the criminals get what they deserve, especially Monks, Fagin and Sykes and that it is possible to change, as shown by Charley Bates.
Sympathy for Nancy, who is given a voice to express her sense of her own guilt and her fate at the hands of Sykes.	Nancy's part in recapturing Oliver, her support of Bill Sykes, despite knowing what he is capable of, and her refusal of the opportunity to reform offered by Rose Maylie.
The use of the middle-class, naïve Oliver to explore the criminal underworld, making the criminals seem appealing and giving a sense of how easy it would be to become a criminal.	Oliver's involvement showing that it is possible not to be corrupted into criminality and a sense that the criminal underworld (however thrilling and entertaining it may be to read about) poses a threat to law-abiding society.

07 Brighton Rock

AO2 Focus might be on:

- beginning and ending;
- use of climaxes, relating to morality and justice;
- the third person narrative – detached yet omniscient;
- shifting focus between characters, especially Ida and Pinkie;
- use of religious language, including Latin;
- descriptive language;
- use of slang in dialogue.

AO3 Focus might be on:

- the setting in 1930s Brighton, its superficial glamour and materialism;
- the criminal underworld, the world of the racecourse and gang warfare;
- the poverty of Rose and Pinkie's background;
- the importance of Catholic beliefs and traditions, giving Pinkie the chance of being saved;
- ideas of heaven and hell;
- Catholics ('Romans') seen as being apart from the rest of British society;
- the ineffectiveness of the police, with the suspicion that of corruption;
- the moral, didactic aspect of the novel.

AO4 Focus might be on:

- the role of Ida as amateur detective and champion of justice;
- the interest in the psychology of the criminal;
- the ending with Pinkie punished (possibly eternally) and Rose saved;
- tension between the law, as represented by Prewitt and the police, and moral justice.

AO5

You might have focussed on some of the following ideas:

For the proposition	Against the proposition
The distinction Greene makes between 'right and wrong' and 'good and evil'.	The difficulty of understanding what this difference is in the context of the novel and whether it is a valid distinction.
The way in which Ida holds to a secular, instinctive idea of justice, albeit based on the Old Testament 'eye for an eye'.	Ida's biblical reference as a reflection of the idea that British culture and the justice system are rooted in Christian morality.
Pinkie and Rose's imperfect understanding of, but belief in, God's judgement and the possibility of divine forgiveness.	Ideas about justice being central to religious morality.
The idea of mortal sin, including marrying outside the church and other acts that are not illegal, as well as murder.	The idea that while there are many sins that are not illegal, most criminal offences are also against the Commandments and so are both illegal and immoral.
The fact that Pinkie is not arrested or tried, so that justice is not officially done.	Pinkie's death being a just outcome in the eyes of Ida and others ('an eye for an eye').
The importance of forgiveness, shown by the confessional scene at the end.	

AO4: The exam board says that you should write about the set texts 'through the lens of crime writing', so make sure you maintain focus on this aspect of the text. This should not be a problem if you stick to the question – most of them will contain a reference to 'crime' or 'criminals'.

08 *The Murder of Roger Ackroyd*

AO2 Focus might be on:

- beginning and ending;
- new revelations in each chapter, building up to the final revelation;
- the set piece when Poirot reveals the characters' crimes;
- use of the unreliable narrator;
- use of Caroline, reflecting curiosity in the village and increasing the reader's curiosity;
- the role of Poirot, the cool, logical outsider;
- use of straightforward language.

AO3 Focus might be on:

- the setting in 1920s small town in rural England, apparently settled and peaceful;
- the country house, a typical setting for a 'locked door' mystery;
- middle-class, apparently respectable society, with its manners and rituals (mah jong, dressing for dinner etc);
- tensions based on class and money.

AO4 Focus might be on:

- the private detective who is a regular in the author's novels and will be expected to solve the crime;
- the detective novel enjoyed as a puzzle by readers;
- middle-class society hiding crime and corruption under a cloak of respectability;
- Sheppard's apparent role as Poirot's assistant (replacing Hastings) and narrator in the manner of Dr Watson, used to trick the reader;
- a sense of justice being done but not via official channels.

AO5

You might have focussed on some of the following ideas:

For the proposition	Against the proposition
The novel as a puzzle to be solved, possibly by the reader, who, paradoxically might be more satisfied by **not** guessing correctly and therefore admiring the cleverness of the plot.	The frustration that might be felt by some who think the solution is somehow unfair and that they have not been given enough clues by the author.
The sense that justice must be done and the right person punished.	A sense that the murderer gets away without a proper trial or punishment.
The restoration of order the discovery brings to a society that has been disrupted and exposed by the crime.	Poirot's complicity in helping the town to avoid scandal, by letting Sheppard kill himself, and a sense that the society of King's Abbot needs to change.

The fact that the revelation, and Poirot's almost priest-like bestowal of forgiveness, helps other characters to move on and have happy endings.	Some readers' feelings that this happiness – like the characters – has no great depth and therefore is not satisfying.
How the final revelation gives insight into the psychology of the murderer and others.	A sense that Sheppard's motive may be less than convincing and that the 'trick' of the plot has prevented readers getting real insight into his mind.

09 *Hamlet*

AO2 Focus might be on:

- beginning and ending;
- use of climaxes relating to the supernatural and Hamlet's 'criminal' actions;
- the appearance of the ghost;
- Hamlet's soliloquies, revealing his motivation;
- the play within a play;
- language and imagery.

AO3 Focus might be on:

- beliefs about ghosts;
- the idea of the divine right of kings;
- religious beliefs about judgement and damnation;
- the revenge tragedy genre;
- biblical prohibition of taking one's brother's wife;
- the society of the court and Hamlet's position in it.

AO4 Focus might be on:

- the cycle of violence and multiple killers set up by the ghost's appearance;
- Hamlet's roles as victim, criminal, detective, avenger and executioner;
- his psychology and motives explored in his soliloquies.

AO5

You might have focussed on some of the following ideas:

For the proposition	Against the proposition
The ghost as a catalyst for everything that happens, as Hamlet discovers what Claudius has done and feels obliged to avenge his father's death.	Whether revenge is necessary or just, whether killing Claudio is indeed a crime, and whether the ghost's appearance is simply a dramatic way of getting him the information about the murder of his father.
Hamlet's actions arising from a sense of divine justice, Claudius's sins being against God, who anointed Hamlet's father and whose laws he has broken.	The idea that, apart from the killing of Claudius, his other 'crimes' have little or nothing to do with justice or religion and whether they are crimes at all (the deaths of Laertes and Polonius are accidental, and he cannot be held directly responsible for Ophelia's death).
The recognition that 'there are more things in heaven and earth' disturbing his mind and causing him to act out of character.	The question of Hamlet's 'madness' and whether it is his disturbed mind that causes the appearance of the ghost and his killings are the result of mental disturbance.

AO5: Every question starts with a statement. Get into the habit of 'interrogating' the question, identifying key words and asking what is meant in the context of your text by, for example, justice, victim or crime.

Section C

10

AO2 Focus might be on:

- the text's form of drama, poetry or prose;
- the use of narrators – Peter Grimes's and the ancient mariner's consciences; the detached narrator in *Brighton Rock*; the 'tricks' played by the narrative in *Atonement*.
- the use of structural features to draw attention to ideas about sin and morality.
- the use of imagery in 'Peter Grimes' and *The Ancient Mariner*.
- religious language in 'Peter Grimes', *The Ancient Mariner*, *Brighton Rock* and *Hamlet*.

AO3 Focus might be on:

- settings (time and place) – Brighton as heaven and hell; the contrast between Fagin's 'kens' and the homes of Mr Brownlow and Miss Maylie;
- social – the dark underworld of *Oliver Twist*; the contrast between the middle-class milieu of Edinburgh and the violent lives of the criminal classes in *When Will There Be Good News?*

- moral – the didactic nature of *Brighton Rock* and *Peter Grimes*; the moral relativism of *When Will There Be Good News?*
- religious – the strong element of religious teaching in *Brighton Rock*, *The Ancient Mariner* and 'Peter Grimes'.

AO4 Focus might be on:
- ideas about revenge – *Hamlet*, *Brighton Rock*, *When Will There Be Good News?*;
- sexual morality – *Oliver Twist*, *Brighton Rock*, *Hamlet*, *Atonement*;
- guilty consciences – *Atonement*, *Brighton Rock*, 'Peter Grimes';
- detectives as moral arbiters – *The Murder of Roger Ackroyd*, *When Will There Be Good News?*;
- moral judgements by society – *Oliver Twist*, *The Murder of Roger Ackroyd*, 'Peter Grimes';
- characters with no sense of morality – Browning's dramatic monologues, Fagin, Dr Sheppard.

AO5

You might have developed any of the above points, suggesting what meanings arise from those ideas and how readers might react, for example:
- Browning, Crabbe and Wilde – the Duke, the woman in the laboratory and Porphyria's killer showing little or no sense of sin or awareness of morality in their narratives; Browning leaving it to readers to consider their actions in the light of morality; Peter Grimes himself and the narrator seeing his actions in term of sin, specifically Christian terms; in *The Ballad of Reading Gaol*, punishment dwelt on more than sin but with a sense that the prisoners have acted immorally.
- Coleridge – Christian symbolism; the mariner's awareness of his sin; his punishment for doing something morally wrong.
- Atkinson – 21st century relative morality; no sense of sin except from Decker whose religion is cynically exploited by Jo Hunter; morality based on emotions; women as arbiters of morality and men as transgressors.
- McEwan – religious connotations of title; Briony's conscience; her absolute morality in reaction to the letter contrasting with her willingness to lie.
- Dickens – assumed sense of right and wrong based on Christian morality; the importance of forgiveness; moral hypocrisy of characters such as Bumble; ideas about sexual morality explored through Nancy and Agnes; good winning in the end.
- Greene – dominated by a sense of sin; ideas about whether Pinkie has a conscience or only knows about sin in theory; mercy and forgiveness; Ida's ideas of right and wrong.
- Christie – assumed morality of English middle classes; most characters having guilty secrets; lack of religious aspect but Poirot 'playing God'; questions about whether Sheppard has a moral sense.
- Shakespeare – Christian morality; religious references; questions over the morality of revenge; seriousness of Claudius's (and Gertrude's) sin; idea of Denmark being 'rotten', having lost its morality.

11

AO2 Focus might be on:
- the text's form of drama, poetry or prose;
- the use of narrators – the 'tricks' played by the narratives of *Atonement* and *The Murder of Roger Ackroyd*;
- the use of structural features to draw attention to ideas about secrecy and betrayal – a new secret being revealed in most chapters of the second half of *The Murder of Roger Ackroyd*;
- the use of dialogue to conceal rather than reveal.

AO3 Focus might be on:
- settings (time and place) – the dark places of Dickens's London and Greene's Brighton; the veneer of middle class respectability in *Atonement*, *When Will There Be Good News?* and *The Murder of Roger Ackroyd* concealing secrets and lies;
- social – the gang culture of *Oliver Twist* and *Brighton Rock*, with their emphasis on loyalty and constant fear of betrayal;
- moral – adultery as a betrayal in *The Murder of Roger Ackroyd* and 'My Last Duchess';

AO4 Focus might be on:
- guilty secrets – *Atonement*, *Brighton Rock*, *Peter Grimes*;
- secrets kept from spouses – *The Murder of Roger Ackroyd*, *When Will There Be Good News?*, *Oliver Twist*;
- secrets kept for gain – *Oliver Twist*, *The Murder of Roger Ackroyd*;
- betrayal of trust – *Atonement*, 'Porphyria's Lover', 'My Last Duchess';
- secret identities – *Oliver Twist*, *When Will There Be Good News?*, *The Murder of Roger Ackroyd*;
- betrayal for a good purpose – *Oliver Twist*, *Brighton Rock*.

AO5

You might have developed any of the above points, suggesting what meanings arise from those ideas and how readers might react, for example:
- Browning, Crabbe and Wilde – the Duke thinking the Duchess has betrayed him; the secret nature of poison; the narrator's betrayal of Porphyria; Peter Grimes keeping secrets and betraying the trust of his victims.
- Coleridge – the mariner's betrayal of his shipmates by killing the albatross.
- Atkinson – Jo's husband keeping secrets from her; Billy keeping secrets from Reggie; husbands betraying their wives; Brodie being betrayed by his new wife, who has kept her identity secret; secret new identities for victims of crime.
- McEwan – Briony's act as a betrayal of her sister; living with the secret for years after the act; keeping the secret even at the end for Paul Marshall and Lola.
- Dickens – Oliver's true identity kept secret; Nancy's betrayal of Oliver and then of the gang; the stress placed on loyalty by Fagin; Noah's betrayal of Fagin.

- Greene – gang culture and a series of betrayals of one gang to another; Pinkie's worry about being betrayed, especially by Rose; his willingness to betray others; Fred's secret identity and secretive job; the secrets of the confessional.
- Christie – Miss Russell's secret child; Ralph and Ursula's secret marriage; Mrs Akroyd's and Flora's secret financial problems; Mrs Ferrars's betrayal of her husband; the secret blackmailing; the pervading atmosphere of gossip; the ultimate secret being the concealment of the murderer's identity.
- Shakespeare – the betrayal of Hamlet's father by his brother and wife; Hamlet's secret plan to catch Claudius and reveal his secret; his betrayal of Ophelia's love; his betrayal by Rosencrantz and Guildenstern.

Paper 2A is an 'open book' exam, meaning you will have your set texts with you. You are expected to quote accurately. You should be able to find quotations you haven't memorised easily by now. If you can't find one quickly, however, don't get bogged down in the search. Paraphrase or use a different quotation.

Paper 2B

Texts and Genres: Elements of Political and Social Protest

For **AO1,** the examiners are looking for the same things for all questions (1–11):
- quality of argument;
- organisation of ideas;
- use of appropriate concepts and terminology;
- technical accuracy.

Section A

01

AO1: Make sure that every point you make is rooted firmly in the text, avoiding speculation and generalisation. Use plenty of short, embedded quotations to illustrate your points.

AO2 Focus might be on:
- omniscient, detached narrator;
- use of the present tense;
- quasi scientific/academic tone (explanatory);
- use of the passive voice, making it seem less personal and more objective ('is expected');
- use of capital letters for key official concepts ('Newspeak', 'the Party');
- use of detailed lists of examples;
- occasional short sentences for impact ('But stupidity is not enough.');
- repetition of 'A Party member' and 'the Party';
- the use of a generalised 'Party member' rather than a named character.

AO3 Focus might be on:
- the totalitarian world described;
- context of time – an imagined future;
- genre – dystopian/science fiction;
- style of newspaper article or academic paper (written like non-fiction).

AO4 Focus might be on:
- generalised description of what life is like;
- descriptions of violent punishment;
- emphasis on the power of the state;
- implied criticism of the powerful;
- implied sympathy for the oppressed;
- detailed descriptions of how oppression works (manipulation of language etc.).

AO5

You may have developed any of the above points, suggesting what meanings arise from them and how readers might react, for example:
- how, by describing the operation of the state, Orwell sets the scene for possible protest/rebellion;
- the bleakness of his vision of a dystopian future and how it can be related to real totalitarian regimes and/or seen as a warning about the future;
- the importance of freedom of thought and language and how it is denied/manipulated by the powerful.

Section B

Before you choose which text to answer on, think carefully about not only the questions in Section B on the texts you have studied but also the general questions in Section C and which texts give you the most scope for answering those questions.

02 *Songs of Innocence and Experience*

AO2 Focus might be on:

- patterning and mirroring of *Innocence* and *Experience* poems;
- lyric and narrative verse;
- the structure of individual poems and relative complexity of form in *Experience*;
- range of rhyme schemes, metrical patterns etc.;
- use of contrast;
- use of rhyme and rhythm;
- use of repetition;
- use of voices;
- apparent simplicity of language;
- religious symbolism;
- imagery of oppression, imprisonment and violence.

AO3 Focus might be on:

- the use of settings (rural and urban; institutional);
- idealisation of children and childhood;
- political/historical context – French Revolution, Industrial Revolution;
- Romantic ideas about man and nature;
- religious context – Blake's version of Christianity and ideas about the established church;
- ideas about education and treatment of children.

AO4 Focus might be on:

- the presentation of protest through the idea of contrasting states;
- the concern with issues such as child labour and slavery;
- the depiction of organised religion as oppressive and corrupting;
- belief in freedom of the body and the spirit.

AO5

You might have focussed on some of the following ideas:

For the proposition	Against the proposition
How the poems show Blake's belief in the freedom of the human spirit and opposition to anything that limits or destroys freedom.	How the oppression and destruction of the human spirit is not a social and political matter but is a spiritual, even mystical, concept in Blake.
Ideas expressed about the essential goodness and innocence of mankind – and opposition to ideas about original sin – through his depiction of babies and children.	How seeing the states of innocence and experience as opposites (one good, the other bad) is an over-simplification; they should be seen as complementary states.
Concerns with the suffering and oppression brought by experience, shown in a social context, e.g. 'The Little Black Boy', 'The Chimney Sweeper', 'London', 'Holy Thursday'.	The fact that most of the poems do not deal in political or social issues, these being instruments of corruption, not its cause.

03 *Selected Poems* (Harrison)

AO2 Focus might be on:

- circular structure of 'V';
- use of quatrains;
- range of forms – free verse, elegiac verse ('V'), lyrical verse, sonnet form ('Working');
- first person and other voices;
- contrast in language – Standard English, Greek, colloquial and vulgar/obscene language;
- imagery and symbolism;
- use of repetition.

AO3 Focus might be on:

- political and social context of 1980s Britain;
- grammar school education in 1940s/50s;
- personal experience of effects of educational opportunities;
- role of employers in creating social division;
- role of education in maintaining social division;
- Gray's *Elegy* and its influence on 'V'.

AO4 Focus might be on:

- focus on the experience of the lower/working classes;
- idea of giving a voice to the voiceless;
- the use of language to break conventions and possibly shock readers/audiences.

AO5

You might have focussed on some of the following ideas:

For the proposition	Against the proposition
Criticism of the poet's own experience of education and the system's endorsement of class divisions ('Them and [uz]').	His awareness of the benefits of his education and the change in his social status.
Awareness of the way he is perceived by the less well-educated ('V', 'Marked with a D').	His empathy for the working classes, unemployed and uneducated.
Use of language to emphasise differences in class/education, including use of Greek and French.	Use of language for self-deprecation; his enjoyment of colloquial language and use of it in poetry, thereby uniting the social classes.
Criticism of the powerful and their role in creating and maintaining class divisions.	The idea that it is not social class and education in themselves that create divisions but the use the powerful make of their power.

AO1/AO4: You need to demonstrate your understanding of poetic techniques, forms and movements but you must always write about these in terms of the poetry as writing of social and political protest, for example: how is Blake's and Harrison's use of repetition relevant to the idea of protest?

04 *The Kite Runner*

AO2 Focus might be on:

- the novel as a Bildungsroman, tracing the narrator's development;
- use of time shifts;
- changes in setting;
- use of voices;
- the first-person narrator's perspective (male and upper class);
- language used about women and people of different classes.

AO3 Focus might be on:

- divisions between Pashtuns and Hazaras and the overlapping of class and ethnic issues;
- depiction of women's role in society – contrast between Afghanistan and America;
- the war against terrorism in Afghanistan;
- Afghan culture and traditions in America.

AO4 Focus might be on:

- Bildungsroman showing growing awareness of issues;
- the narrator having experience of different societies and being set up as someone (writer) who observes and criticises;
- the use of real historical and political events;
- focus on the effect of political and historical events on individuals;
- the significance of gender and social class in relation to revolution and change in Afghanistan.

AO5

You might have focussed on some of the following ideas:

For the proposition	Against the proposition
How social class is ingrained in Afghan society and shapes relationships, especially the relationship between Amir and Hassan.	How the difference between the boys is as much ethnic as class-based; Pashtuns regard themselves as superior to Hazaras and employ them as servants; how this is different from European/American ideas about class.
The position of women in Afghanistan at the beginning, where they can dress and behave like westerners, compared to their life under the Taliban.	How women are not prominent in the novel and the narrative voice is that of a man, so they are seen primarily in relation to him.
How these freedoms, like so many other things, are only enjoyed by upper and middle classes, shown in the story of Hassan's mother.	Amir's mother being as privileged as he is, because of her ethnicity; Hassan's mother being oppressed partly because of hers.
The significance of social class: Amir and his father's new life in America and how traditional attitudes to class (emphasis on family background; the general's attitude to Sohrab) and gender (Soraya's shame) continue but are starting to change in the Afghan community.	The general's attitude to Sohrab being because of his ethnic background; he and Amir's father remaining proud of being Pashtuns and not part of the American class system; Afghans as an ethnic minority in America and their experience being that of immigrant.

05 *Harvest*

AO2 Focus might be on:

- the historical novel used to explore present-day concerns;
- short time-span showing rapid change;
- use of analepsis (flashback) to give sense of society;
- use of first person narrator – position as outsider and possible naivety;
- other voices;
- biblical language;
- language that is not contemporary but not archaic either;
- language used about women and people of different classes;
- use of the present tense – immediacy.

AO3 Focus might be on:

- setting in an imprecise, non-industrial past;
- idea of England;
- ideas about rural idylls and biblical ideas of Eden before the fall;
- context of present day tensions between nationalism and internationalism/globalisation;
- the historical reality of enclosures;
- the economic ideas of Jordan with his possibly anachronistic mantra of 'Profit, Progress and Enterprise'.

AO4 Focus might be on:

- emphasis on the harm done by capitalism;
- how the novel plays on nostalgia but rejects it, showing the harshness of life in the past;
- the effect of political and historical events on individuals.

AO5

You might have focussed on some of the following ideas:

For the proposition	Against the proposition
How the society of the village appears peaceful and secure – almost idyllic – but the narrator is aware of how this comes from its remoteness.	How the village's problems derive more from its backwardness (which is exacerbated by its remoteness) than by its isolation as such.
Reaction to the newcomers, their scapegoating and how their treatment shows the ruthlessness with which a society can strive to protect its own people.	The subplot of the Beldame family being more about suspicion of foreigners and prejudice than about being isolated, and having little or nothing to do with the changes Jordan makes.
Jordan's new ideas, his determination to change things and his capitalism.	The changes in the village being unrelated to industrialisation, recalling the enclosure of common land in the 17th and 18th century.
The way in which the village's old way of life is doomed in the face of progress.	A sense that the village's destruction is not inevitable; that Kent's weakness and mistakes made by the villagers are contributory factors.
How events and attitudes in the novel might make the reader think about 21st century issues, such as isolationism, nationalism and globalisation.	The vagueness of not only the setting but also its politics and the futility of applying anything therein to real life issues.

AO3/AO5: Context includes the context of how texts are received. Beware of assuming that all 21st century readers will bring the same ideas and assumptions and react in the same way. Look up reviews on the internet and talk to other people who have read the books to stimulate thought and provide different perspectives.

06 *Hard Times*

AO2 Focus might be on:

- use of the industrial novel to explore education;
- changes of scene and contrasts between scenes (e.g. the school and the circus);
- beginning and ending;
- the three-part structure;
- the intrusive narrator making the writer's views clear;
- use of humour;
- detailed descriptions;
- use of rhetorical and hyperbolic language;
- use of dialogue to explore issues.

AO3 Focus might be on:

- setting in industrial Lancashire;
- the power and responsibilities of local industrialists and politicians;

- theories of education and child development satirised;
- the organisation of education in Victorian Britain (novel written before compulsory education);
- illiteracy of many adults;
- child labour;
- 19th century interest in expanding scientific knowledge and economics;
- the importance of creativity and entertainment.

AO4 Focus might be on:

- satirical tone, enabling the writer to criticise and express anger through humour;
- sympathy for the oppressed, often slipping into sentimentality;
- focus on the effects of industrialisation and capitalism on individuals;
- Dickens's reputation as a campaigner on social issues.

AO5

You might have focussed on some of the following ideas:

For the proposition	Against the proposition
The importance of education to Gradgrind and Bounderby, its place in the life of Coketown and its centrality to the novel.	The lack of relevance of education to most of Coketown's inhabitants and the goodness and nobility seen in the uneducated Stephen.
The damage done by their narrow view of education, particularly to Louisa but also to Bitzer, who sticks rigidly to their ideas and Sissy, who is considered a failure because of her inability to fit into the 'System'.	The view that Louisa is not damaged by the System so much as by a lack of parental love, of which the System is a symptom not a cause; that Sissy is unaffected by her lack of educational success; and that Bitzer has been enabled to achieve.
The Coketown version of education as a product of the narrow and inhuman philosophy of the industrialists.	The way in which the satire shows us a bad education, belittling the importance of 'ologies' and mathematics, for example, and perhaps implying that no education is better than that given by the M'Choakumchilds.
Glimpses of what a more creative child-centred education might be, for example: Louisa and Tom's curiosity about the circus; Sissy's learning to read through fiction; Louisa's attitude to children at the end.	The failure to present a meaningful and developed version of a 'good' education so that we only see education as society's failure (is there an implication even that poor people would be happier without education and would 'know their place' unlike Bitzer and Slackbridge?).

AO4: The exam board says that you should write about the set texts 'through the lens of political and social protest writing' so make sure you maintain focus on this aspect of the text. This should not be a problem if you read the question properly and stick to it.

07 *Henry IV Part 1*

AO2 Focus might be on:

- beginning with England suffering the effects of the deposition of Richard II;
- plot following the pursuit of power by Hotspur, Worcester and others;
- contrast between Henry's statesman-like language and Hotspur's violent, immoderate language;
- imagery of, for example, violent weather, bloodshed;
- Falstaff's comic subplot;
- story structure of exposition, development, denouement and resolution;
- use of different settings;
- visual power of battle scenes.

AO3 Focus might be on:

- belief in the divine right of kings;
- questions over the legitimacy of Henry's claim to the throne and the Tudor version of history;
- the background of the events of *Richard II*;
- the power of the noble families;
- the threats from Scotland and Wales and their reputation for barbarism;
- the importance of father/son relationships.

AO4 Focus might be on:

- instability of the state and the unknown potential results of rebellion;
- the text seen as supporting the status quo and the restoration of it at the end, whatever the rights and wrongs of Henry's claim;
- the appeal of rebellious characters like Hotspur.

AO5

You might have focussed on some of the following ideas:

For the proposition	Against the proposition
The act of rebellion as destabilising and dangerous, whatever its justification; the rebels' motives as disingenuous (they have decided that Henry is not the rightful king despite helping him become King) and selfish.	Henry's deposition of an anointed king, which was an act of sacrilege as well as of rebellion, being responsible for creating a destabilised and dangerous kingdom.
The rebels being shown as dangerous because of temperament (Hotspur), superstition (Glendower), wildness (Douglas) and untrustworthiness (Worcester) while Henry appears statesman-like and forgiving, with Hal a brave and worthy successor.	The idea that the possession of power in itself creates danger – Hal's rebellion alerts us to the danger of giving power to those who cannot use it responsibly; Falstaff, given a small amount of power, abuses it; the rebels could be seen as abusing the power they already have to plunge the country into war.

08 *A Doll's House*

AO2 Focus might be on:

- three-act structure;
- story structure of exposition, development, denouement and resolution;
- unity of time, space and action;
- setting the same throughout – domestic, middle class, respectable;
- time – three days over Christmas;
- use of voices/dialogue;
- manners of the time and class reflected in dialogue.

AO3 Focus might be on:

- respectability of 19th century middle-class Norway;
- the importance of money/financial issues;
- gender roles/patriarchy;
- influence of 19th century feminist movements;
- the shocked reaction to the play on first performance;
- differences in audience assumptions then and now.

AO4 Focus might be on:

- Nora's rebellion against ideas of respectability and her feeling that her married life is a pretence;
- Helmer's concern about what Nora's actions look like to society rather than whether they are right or wrong;
- the importance to Krogstad of his reputation (his career and income depending on it) as a driver of the plot;
- the exposure of the shallowness of the outward respectable reputations of others.

AO5

You might have focussed on some of the following ideas:

For the proposition	Against the proposition
The title of the play and how Nora's marriage is in some ways a childish game but also a constant struggle to keep up appearances, for example by getting into debt.	Nora's powerlessness coming mainly from her position as a woman in a patriarchal society and her dependency on first her father and then her husband.
The revelation that, after Nora's agonising about the effect on her marriage of financial affairs, Helmer is concerned mainly about his reputation being intact.	How the situation is of her own making – Helmer has a decent job; it is not clear whether he really needed the holiday for his health; she has no trouble employing two servants and can be extravagant.
The freedom Nora finds (paradoxically) in dressing up to dance the tarantella, which is short-lived, however, and controlled by Helmer.	The tarantella as a sign that Nora is not completely powerless – her passion and her sexuality are powerful forces.
A growing awareness of how the lives of others are controlled by the need to preserve their reputations and its consequences for individuals (Krogstad's desperation to save his career; Mrs Linde's loveless marriage; Anne-Marie's child; Dr Rank's inherited disease; Nora's father's profligacy).	How other characters have not allowed themselves to be defeated by reputation and appearances – Krogstad and Mrs Linde look like having a happy ending together; Anne-Marie's child has a happy life and she has moved on (ironically looking after Nora's children); Dr Rank has had a good life and dies as he wishes.

09 *The Handmaid's Tale*

AO2 Focus might be on:

- dystopian form;
- first-person narrative;

- fictional diary/autobiography;
- academic commentary in last chapter;
- chronology including flashbacks and time jumps;
- awareness of process of memory and reconstruction;
- biblical language and imagery.

AO3 Focus might be on:

- Christian/biblical context;
- links with Puritan society of 17th century America;
- links to slavery in America;
- parallels with Iran, Afghanistan, Romania;
- awareness of 1970s/80s feminism
- awareness of the 'religious right' in late 20th century America;
- environmental issues in the 20th century;
- 21st century concerns about issues of identity politics, free speech and the tensions between them.

AO4 Focus might be on:

- ideas of what is a feminist work of literature (see Atwood's introduction);
- focus on oppression and rebellion in dystopian novels set in the future;
- the use of the first-person narrator giving voice to the oppressed;
- focus on the experience of women;
- relevance of the novel to various forms of oppression and various societies.

AO5

You might have focussed on some of the following ideas:

For the proposition	Against the proposition
The act of writing as a form of rebellion by Offred.	The novel as an account of life in Gilead/Offred's personal story and not a means of protest.
The growing awareness of the extent of rebellion against the regime (by Moira, Ofglen and Nick as well as by groups such as the Baptists).	The futility of rebelling against the regime, shown in the executions and disappearances, and by the historian's account of what happened afterwards.
Descriptions of small acts of domestic rebellion, not only by Offred but also by the Commander, Serena Joy and the previous Offred.	How small acts of rebellion only demonstrate how oppressive the regime is.
Flashbacks focussing on feminist campaigns of the late 20th century and on Offred's mother.	Feminism seen as unsuccessful or even as contributing to a climate of oppression.
Rebellion against sexual oppression and the denial of emotions by Offred, Nick and the Commander.	The state's success in repressing and controlling sexuality, seen in the treatment of Janine, the Ceremony and Jezebel's.

AO5: Every question starts with a statement. Get into the habit of 'interrogating' the question, identifying key words and asking what is meant in the context of your text by, for example, servitude, rebellion, oppression or protest.

Section C

10

AO2 Focus might be on:

- the text's form of drama, poetry or prose;
- the use of narrators – the first-person narrator in *The Handmaid's Tale*; the intrusive narrator in *Hard Times*;
- structure – three distinct parts of *The Kite Runner* showing the impact of oppression;
- the use of poetic form to emphasise oppression – repetition in Blake and Harrison;
- language of oppression in *Harvest*, *The Handmaid's Tale*;
- imagery.

AO3 Focus might be on:

- settings (time and place) – Afghanistan under the Taliban in *The Kite Runner*; the school and factory in *Hard Times*;
- social – the feudal village in *Harvest*, Afghan tradition and customs in *The Kite Runner*;
- moral – Blake's representation of child labour, slavery etc.; Amir's treatment of Hassan and the Taliban's treatment of children in *The Kite Runner*;
- historical – feminist movements of the 19th (*A Doll's House*) and 20th (*The Handmaid's Tale*) centuries; the Poor Law and industrialisation (*Hard Times*); working class history, divisions in 20th century Britain in Harrison.

AO4 Focus might be on:

- oppression of working people – *Hard Times*, *Harvest*, Harrison;
- oppression of women – *The Handmaid's Tale*, *A Doll's House*;

- oppression on ethnic grounds – *The Kite Runner*, *Songs of Innocence and Experience*;
- oppression of the spirit – Harrison, *Songs of Innocence and Experience*, *Hard Times*;
- oppression of individuality – *The Handmaid's Tale*, *Hard Times*, *A Doll's House*;
- relations between masters/servants – *The Kite Runner*, *The Handmaid's Tale*, *Hard Times*, *Harvest*;
- portrayals of servants in minor roles – *A Doll's House*, *Henry IV Part 1*.

AO5

You may have developed any of the above points, suggesting what meanings arise from them and how readers might react, for example:
- Blake – many forms of oppression shown in 'Songs of Experience', both social and spiritual; the yearning for innocence and freedom; oppression being man-made; institutions such as church and state as instruments of oppression; servitude as part of human life.
- Harrison – oppression of workers/children in 'Working'; oppression of the unemployed/the young in 'V'; oppression/denial of regional/working class identity in 'Them and [uz]', 'V', 'National Trust'.
- Hosseini – the awkward relationship between Amir and Hassan due to Hassan being a servant; the oppression of Hazaras by Pashtans accepted as the norm; the greater oppression of all Afghans by the Taliban; the servitude of women and children; Amir's awareness of his privilege and feelings of guilt.
- Crace – the feudal nature of the village society and the villagers' apparent contentment with it; Walter's ambiguous position as Kent's former servant and his loyalty; the more overt oppression of the village by Jordan; Jordan's use of violence to enforce his power; the villagers' inability to resist.
- Dickens – the servitude of the factory hands; the attitude of Bounderby towards them; their attempts to resist; the Union seen as oppressive; the oppression of creativity and childhood through education; Stephen crushed by oppression and servitude.
- Atwood – the title; Offred's subservient position and her name; the rigid stratification of society in Gilead; women as servants of men and of each other; the Guardians' servitude (Nick as the Commander's servant).
- Ibsen – the 'doll's house' as a prison; Nora oppressed by the norms and expectations of society; Helmer and Krogstad as servants of the bank and capitalism; the two actual servants barely noticed.
- Shakespeare – the rebellion not the result of oppression; servitude present in the sense of all subjects being servants of the King; portrayal of mostly cheerful, comic characters in serving roles.

11

AO2 Focus might be on:

- the text's form of drama, poetry or prose;
- the use of narrators – the narrators' awareness of their class in *Harvest*, *The Handmaid's Tale* and *The Kite Runner*, Harrison; Dickens's comments on class in *Hard Times*;
- structure – Nora's debts driving the plot in *A Doll's House*;
- dialogue – different language used by characters from different classes in *Hard Times* and Harrison;
- contrasts in settings – wealthy Kabul/poor America in *The Kite Runner*, the court/the tavern in *Henry IV Part 1*;
- visual impact of set in *A Doll's House*, showing social status;
- recurring references to money in *A Doll's House*, *Hard Times*, *The Kite Runner*, *Harvest*, *Henry IV Part 1*.

AO3 Focus might be on:

- settings (time and place) – suburban luxury in Kabul/flea markets in America in *The Kite Runner;* Stephen's home/Bounderby's homes in *Hard Times*; the manor house in *Harvest;* contemporary urban settings in Harrison's poems;
- social – the feudal village in *Harvest*; Afghan tradition and customs in *The Kite Runner*; differences between the classes in *Hard Times*; male working-class society in Harrison;
- moral – Amir's sense of guilt in *The Kite Runner;* the emotive way poverty is depicted in *Hard Times*, *Henry IV Part 1*, *A Doll's House*, *The Kite Runner*; implied immorality of capitalism in *Harvest*;
- historical – acceptance of differences in wealth and class in *Henry IV Part 1* and by characters in *Harvest*; attitudes to money in *A Doll's House* and *Hard Times;* unemployment and poverty in Harrison.

AO4 Focus might be on:

- differences in wealth and social class – Harrison, *Hard Times*, *Harvest*, *Henry IV Part 1*, *The Kite Runner*;
- portrayal/discussion of capitalism – Harrison, *Harvest*, *Hard Times*, *A Doll's House*;
- conflict arising from differences in class/wealth – Harrison, *Hard Times*;
- portrayals of poverty – Harrison, *Songs of Innocence and Experience*, *Hard Times*, *The Kite Runner*;
- movement between social classes – Harrison, *The Kite Runner*, *Hard Times*.

AO5

- Blake – differences in social class not shown; portrayals of poverty ('The Chimney Sweeper', 'London'); focus not on differences between people but on common humanity and spiritual, not financial or class-based concerns.
- Harrison – poet's awareness of his own class; changing ideas of 'working class' and distinctions within 'working class' from child labour through tradesmen/skilled workers to the unemployed; emphasis on the effect of poverty on communities and individuals.
- Hosseini – the narrator very conscious of his family's wealth and the contrast between their house and Hassan's hut; Afghan society class-ridden but social class related to ethnicity; descent into poverty of Afghans in exile but their retention of a sense of their class; some sense of how differences in wealth may have caused revolutions; poverty and wealth in modern Afghanistan.

- Crace – the feudal nature of the village society and the villagers' apparent contentment with it; the villagers' creation of an underclass with the Beldames; wealth and capitalist ideas of Jordan; differences in class meaning that the villagers are powerless.
- Dickens – vivid but sentimental depiction of poverty; contrast with Bounderby's wealth; Bounderby's pride in his fictional rise from poverty (although his real beginnings are still humble); Stephen oppressed by people of his own class as well as the wealthy.
- Atwood – wealth in the hands of the ruling classes; contrast between Wives and Econowives; removal of women's financial independence; rigid class system of Gilead.
- Ibsen – most of characters belong to the same social class; there is no tension between Nora and her maids; security and comfort important to all; a dread of poverty; both Krogstad and Nora creating their own financial problems; audiences possibly having more sympathy with Mrs Linde than with Nora.
- Shakespeare – social class and wealth not issues in the text; lower-class characters as 'lovable rogues' and comic characters; their scenes providing contrast to the court scenes.

And finally … try to look on your exams as an opportunity rather than an ordeal. You've been given two and a half or three hours in a peaceful environment to express your ideas about texts you've studied and (let's hope) enjoyed. Here are the two best pieces of advice I've ever been given about sitting exams:
- **Don't 'cram' the night before; eat properly, get some fresh air and have a good night's sleep.**
- **RTBQ (Read the Bloody Question)!**

Practice Exam 2

A-level English Literature B

Mark scheme

For the mark scheme for all questions (Papers 1A, 1B, 2A and 2B) please see pages 55–56.

Paper 1A

Literary Genres: Aspects of Tragedy

For **AO1**, the examiners are looking for the same things for all questions (1–8):

- quality of argument;
- organisation of ideas;
- use of appropriate concepts and terminology;
- technical accuracy.

AO1: Accurate spelling, punctuation and grammar are important – and not just because they're marked. Poor technical skills inhibit understanding of what you have written. When revising, look again at any punctuation or spelling issues you may be unsure about.

01 *Othello*

AO2 Focus might be on:

- the scene's position in the play as the tragedy reaches its climax;
- the position of this extract just after the shock of Desdemona's death;
- the visual impact of the scene – Desdemona's body, Othello's commanding presence;
- the violent/emotional language;
- contrast with the gentle/affectionate language to Desdemona;
- Othello's use of rhetorical questions and exclamations;
- reference to hell and devils;
- change in mood/tone in dialogue with Lodovico;
- the impact of the sudden violence of wounding Iago.

AO3 Focus might be on:

- the setting in Desdemona's bedroom;
- ideas about marriage and relationships between men and women;
- notions of honour;
- religious ideas about damnation and biblical allusions;
- ideas about fate;
- the background of war and Othello's status as general.

AO4 Focus might be on:

- Othello's death as the climax of the play;
- his stature as a tragic hero;
- the role of Iago in engineering Othello's tragedy;
- the role of minor characters such as Lodovico in bringing the play to an end and restoring order.

AO5:

You could develop any of the points made above and suggest different meanings arising from them as well as audience reactions, for example:

- how the extract shows the tragic result of Othello's flaws and Iago's plotting;
- how audiences' sympathies might shift between Desdemona and Othello;
- Othello's confused emotions and reactions and the audience's interpretation of them: grief, pity, defiance, calm, pride, anger, self-justification.

02 *King Lear*

AO2 Focus might be on:

- the structural importance of the scene – the resolution of the Gloucester subplot;
- the revelations about Kent and Goneril and Regan as part of the build-up to the play's climax;
- Edgar's long narrative speech;
- Edgar's language in contrast with his language as Poor Tom;
- Edgar's use of exclamations breaking up his speech to show emotion ('O fault!');
- change in mood signalled by the entrance of the Gentleman;
- visual impact of the bloody knife;
- use of questions by Albany and Edmund to elicit information.

AO3 Focus might be on:

- context of civil war;
- setting in an army camp on the eve of battle;
- ideas about kingship, the divine right of kings and Lear's abandonment of his role;
- Albany's command of the army, his authority coming through his wife;
- ideas about families – divisions between parents and children, and between brothers;
- the way in which this discord reflects the discord of the country and is against the natural order.

AO4 Focus might be on:

- the use of the Gloucester subplot to mirror Lear's story and intensify the tragedy;
- the involvement of others in the tragic hero's fall and their deaths;
- the eventual resolution of plot strands and the restoration of order;
- the bloodbath that often comes at the end of 17th century tragedy;
- a sense of the downfall of the powerful and hubristic;
- tragedy invoking reactions of pity and sorrow in the audience, reflected in the reactions of characters.

AO5

You could develop any of the points made above and suggest different meanings arising from them as well as audience reactions, for example:

- the rather mechanical nature of the scene, dealing with revelations and resolutions, and its role in building up the climax of the tragedy;
- the function and importance of the Gloucester subplot with its parent/child relationships mirroring those of Lear and his daughters as Gloucester's misjudgement of Edgar mirrors Lear's of Cordelia;
- the significance of honest/virtuous characters such as Edgar, Albany and Kent in a chaotic, disordered world;
- the significance of disguise thematically and in terms of plot.

AO2/AO4: As you're reading the unseen extract, annotate or highlight the text. Look for striking examples of the writer's techniques and for points that relate to ideas about tragedy and themes that are important elsewhere in the play.

03 *Othello*

AO2 Focus might be on:

- Othello's jealousy is placed at the centre of the plot;
- Iago's soliloquies share his plans with the audience;
- Othello's language displays both arrogance and paranoia;
- the visual impact of Othello's fit;
- the symbolism of the handkerchief.

AO3 Focus might be on:

- the role played by Othello's ethnicity;
- Iago's identification with the devils of medieval drama;
- the context of the settings in Venice and Cyprus, and Othello's status;
- Jacobean ideas about chastity, marriage and honour.

AO4 Focus might be on:

- the idea of the 'fatal flaw' in Shakespearean tragedy – Othello's jealousy;
- Othello's 'hubris', which must be punished in classical tragedy;
- Othello depicted as a 'great' man before his fall;
- the element of revenge in Iago's plotting.

AO5

You might have focussed on some of the following ideas:

For the proposition	Against the proposition
Traditional ideas about the tragic hero and how Othello's tragedy fits with them.	Tragic heroes seen as victims of fate and the actions of others.
The ways in which Othello's flaws influence and affect those around him, as well as giving them opportunities to plot against him.	How much Othello's downfall depends on the success of Iago's plot and how the actions of Roderigo, Cassio, Desdemona and Emilia contribute to its success.
The centrality and dominance of Othello as a character; the audience's focus being on his strengths and weaknesses.	The dramatic function of Iago, his interaction with the audience and the sense that Othello's flaws are exacerbated, if not caused, by his deceit.

04 *Othello*

AO2 Focus might be on:

- Othello and Desdemona's elopement and marriage at the start of the play;
- Iago's stated intentions to betray Othello in his soliloquies;

- language of love used by Othello and Desdemona;
- focus on their love at the climax of the play;
- animal imagery associated with sex.

AO3 Focus might be on:

- Desdemona's chastity and fidelity;
- the importance of fidelity in marriage – honour;
- ideas about loyalty to the state, in the army, in relationships;
- marriage for love and against the wishes of Desdemona's father;
- biblical references recalling Adam and Eve's betrayal.

AO4 Focus might be on:

- love leading to jealousy and betrayal, causing the tragedy;
- association of love with death – 'one that lov'd not wisely, but too well'.

AO5

You might have focussed on some of the following ideas:

For the proposition	Against the proposition
The centrality of Othello and Desdemona's love, Othello's jealousy and Iago's use of it to bring about Othello's tragic end.	How it is not their love that causes the tragedy, but Othello's jealousy and pride.
Recurring ideas of betrayal – Iago and Cassio's betrayal of Othello, Emilia's unwitting betrayal of Desdemona, Othello's belief that Desdemona has betrayed him.	What is meant by 'betrayal' – Iago is motivated by revenge, Cassio by ambition, Emilia by a wish to please Iago, while infidelity is a matter of sin and dishonour, not betrayal.
Ideas about the dangers of overpowering love and sexual passion causing irrationality, violence and death.	How love is the one positive emotion present in the play.

05 *King Lear*

AO2 Focus might be on:

- the structural positioning and visual impact of Lear's division of the kingdom;
- the role of the fool in pointing out the foolishness of the powerful;
- the bombast of Lear's early speeches;
- the patterning of his rejection of Cordelia followed by his rejection by Goneril and Regan;
- constant references to madness and folly.

AO3 Focus might be on:

- Jacobean ideas about the divine right of kings;
- the tradition of fools at court;
- the importance of the stability of the state;
- differences between modern and 17th century ideas about absolute power;
- traditions of mockery of the powerful in literature;
- the idea of Britain as a nation, promoted by James I/VI;
- change in settings reflecting instability and division.

AO4 Focus might be on:

- Lear as a tragic hero – his hubris and his fatal flaw;
- catharsis felt by audiences watching the 'great' suffer;
- use of comedy within tragedy;
- the actions of a tragic hero disturbing the natural order.

AO5

You might have focussed on some of the following ideas:

For the proposition	Against the proposition
The importance of themes of madness and folly, especially the fool's commentary on Lear's foolishness and the absurdity of power.	Madness and folly in the powerful as destructive forces.
The way in which the division of the kingdom leads to almost farcical scenes, from Lear's retinue being cut to Goneril and Regan's fight over Edmund.	The destructiveness of the division of the kingdom in terms of its impact on the natural order and the stability of the state.
Consideration of Lear's 'mad scenes' when he is powerless, in comparison with the earlier scenes where his power leads him to absurd behaviour.	Lear's madness as an example of how power, when misused, can destroy the powerful.

06 *King Lear*

AO2 Focus might be on:

- the structural position of his descent into madness;
- the mirroring of his madness in 'Poor Tom';
- the change in his language;
- the apparent disconnectedness of his thoughts;
- interplay with the fool;
- his awareness of his folly at the end of the play.

AO3 Focus might be on:

- 17th century ideas about madness;
- expectations of how a king would behave – the shock of a 'mad' king on stage;
- the importance of the king's stability to the state's stability;
- whether different audiences would react with different degrees of sympathy.

AO4 Focus might be on:

- whether a character can be tragic if he deceives others, including the audience;
- Lear's madness as an essential part of his downfall;
- the idea of catharsis and the need for the audience to share the tragic hero's pain.

AO5

You might have focussed on some of the following ideas:

For the proposition	Against the proposition
How Lear does not become mad until after he has lost all his power and the sympathy of others.	Lear's madness as the nadir of his mental, spiritual and emotional journey, the seeds of which are sown earlier in the play.
The 'mad' Lear being clearly more sympathetic, invoking pity from Edgar, the fool, Kent and Cordelia.	How Edgar, the fool, Kent and Cordelia are already sympathetic to him but have been rejected by him when apparently sane.
The use of pretended madness in the subplot – if Edgar's madness is an illusion, surely Lear's could be too – causing audiences to consider what is meant by madness.	The clear signalling of Edgar's intention to pretend to be mad in his soliloquies, the lack of any such signalling by Lear (which would be expected in 17th century drama) and Edgar and the fool's belief in the reality of Lear's madness.

Your response should be 'informed by different interpretations' (AO5). There is huge body of Shakespearean criticism and you should have considered some of it. It can help to refer to critics by name or to schools of criticism.

Section C

For **AO2** the examiners are looking for the same things in both questions 7 and 8:
- the structure of the drama text in relation to the text;
- the use of dialogue, dramatic action, exits and entrances, soliloquies and flashbacks in the drama text;
- the possible use of a poetry text or a novel and how their methods shape meaning;
- the writers' uses of structural, linguistic and other devices to shape meaning.

07

AO3 Focus might be on:
- ideas about kingship in *Richard II*;
- the idea of the American Dream and the pursuit of wealth in *Death of a Salesman* and *The Great Gatsby*;
- ideas about women and equality in *Tess of the D'Urbervilles* and 'Jessie Cameron';
- the use of classical myth and legend in 'Tithonus' and 'Lamia';
- the Christian/biblical context of *The Monk's Tale* and *Paradise Lost*.

AO4 Focus might be on:

- the concept of a 'tragic hero' and the distinction between heroes and protagonists (who are often just victims);
- the tradition of tragedies ending with a sense of catharsis and restoration of order;
- tragic literature that ends with a sense of waste and a bleak view of the world.

AO5

You might have focussed on some of the following ideas:

For the proposition	Against the proposition
Richard II's failures as king meaning he cannot be trusted with the care of the kingdom; uncertainty about whether Bolingbroke's success will mean an end to war.	Richard II sympathetically portrayed, foolish and proud but not necessarily untrustworthy (it is those around him who are); Bolingbroke's accession giving hope to the nation.
Willy Loman's serial deceit, disappointing himself and his wife, and the sense of waste invoked by his death and its manner.	Willy Loman being foolish rather than untrustworthy; his death as inevitable leaving a sense of catharsis.
Tess's instability and inability to fight victimhood; the opportunities presented for a happy ending.	Tess's tragedy as the result of her innocence, and her trusting nature (it is the men who cannot be trusted); her death as the only satisfactory way for the novel to end.
The mystery of where Gatsby's wealth has originated; the use of Nick as a narrator to distance him and make him unknowable; the sense that his death is absurd and wasteful.	Gatsby's dishonesty being hinted at but not established; his dealings with other characters, including Nick, tending to show him as trustworthy; his death seen almost as punishment for his success.
The uncertainty about who is the tragic figure in 'Lamia' and 'Isabella' – Lamia being untrustworthy; the bleak, unfulfilling endings of 'Isabella' and 'La Belle Dame Sans Merci'.	Keats's protagonists as innocent victims – Lycius, the knight, Isabella.
Lucifer/Satan as the epitome of untrustworthiness in *The Monk's Tale* and *Paradise Lost*; Tithonus as an example of a protagonist who has unsatisfying end; 'Jessie Cameron' leaving readers disappointed that Jessie has not escaped.	The protagonists of 'Miss Gee', 'Death in Leamington', 'Tithonus' and 'Jessie Cameron' seen as victims who have not deceived anyone; the lack of moral satisfaction to be gained from Satan's downfall; a sense of gentle calm about the death in Leamington.

08

AO3 Focus might be on:

- Christian beliefs and traditions in *The Monk's Tale*, *Paradise Lost*, *Richard II* and Keats;
- religion and ideas about sin criticised in *Tess of the D'Urbervilles*;
- changing attitudes to morality in *The Great Gatsby* and *Death of a Salesman*.

AO4 Focus might be on:

- the sense that sins such as pride will be punished as part of tragic experience (*Richard II*, *The Monk's Tale*, *The Great Gatsby*, 'Lamia', 'Tithonus');
- the effects of guilt on the protagonist, allowing audience sympathy (*Tess of the D'Urbervilles*, *Death of a Salesman*);
- the sins of others creating tragic victims ('Isabella', 'The Eve of Saint Agnes', *Tess of the D'Urbervilles*, 'Jessie Cameron', 'The Convergence of the Twain').

AO5

You might have focussed on some of the following ideas:

For the proposition	Against the proposition
Richard's behaviour as king seen as immoral and his death as a punishment; some feelings of guilt about his behaviour; Bolingbroke's actions against an anointed king as serious sins.	Richard's deposition being due to his poor performance as king; his being more interested in cursing Bolingbroke than admitting guilt; Bolingbroke's belief in his right to the crown.
Willy's unfaithfulness and greed seen as sinful; his death as the result of his feelings of guilt.	The lack of a concept of 'sin' in the 20th century America shown in *Death of a Salesman*; Willy's despair due to failure rather than guilt.
Tess's behaviour seen as sinful by the society she lives in, resulting in guilt; Alec's and Angel's behaviour to her seen as sinful; Angel's feelings of guilt; the sin of murder and Tess's punishment for her guilt.	Implicit criticism of the idea of sin in *Tess of the D'Urbervilles*; Tess seemingly absolved from responsibility because of a combination of her position in society and Fate.
Tom and Myrtle's affair seen as sinful; Tom feeling guilty about it; materialism and greed as sinful.	*The Great Gatsby* as a picture of an amoral society, with no sense of sin or guilt.
Cuchulain guilty of his son's death; Lucifer and Adam responsible for bringing sin and misery to the world; Adam's guilt; the guilt and punishment of Tithonus. Lamia's sin and guilt; the sin and guilt of Isabella's brothers.	How a sense of sin and/or guilt varies in Keats according to the setting and the story – La Belle Dame and Lamia having no feelings of guilt; the actions of the knight and Lycius caused by natural feelings that are not defined as sinful. Sin playing no part in the tragedies of 'Miss Gee', 'Death in Leamington' and 'Out, out'; no feelings of guilt expressed in these poems.

AO4 asks you to 'explore connections across literary texts'. The exam board stresses that this should be done in the context of tragedy. Whether you are writing about two texts (Sections A and B) or one (Section C), you need to show that you have studied and understood ideas about tragedy, but you must ensure that everything you say is relevant to the text and the question.

Paper 1B

Literary Genres: Aspects of Comedy

For **AO1** the examiners are looking for the same things for all questions (1–8):

- quality of argument;
- organisation of ideas;
- use of appropriate concepts and terminology;
- technical accuracy.

Accurate spelling, punctuation and grammar are important – and not just because they're marked. Poor technical skills inhibit understanding of what you have written. When revising, look again at any punctuation or spelling issues you may be unsure about.

01 *The Taming of the Shrew*

AO2 Focus might be on:

- the significance of the scene structurally – the beginning of the Lucentio/Bianca subplot;
- contrast between Lucentio's flowery language and Tranio's plain speaking;
- Lucentio's use of references to classical mythology;
- Tranio's subservient status shown in his use of 'master' and 'sir';
- Lucentio's use of hyperbole;
- Tranio's use of Latin, suggesting that he is clever and well-educated;
- Tranio's aside to the audience.

AO3 Focus might be on:

- Elizabethan ideas about marriage;
- conventions of courtship reflected in Lucentio's language;
- use of classical stories;
- the idea of the clever, resourceful servant in literature;
- the authority of fathers over their daughters, especially when choosing husbands;
- changes in ideas about love over time and how they might affect audience reactions.

AO4 Focus might be on:

- use of the subplot to contrast with the main plot of Petruchio and Katherine;
- Lucentio and Bianca providing a more conventional version of romantic comedy;
- Lucentio having to overcome obstacles put in the way of his love for Bianca;
- comedies conventionally beginning with love at first sight and ending with the true lovers marrying;
- the audience being privy to Tranio's plot.

AO5

You could develop any of the points made above and suggest different meanings arising from them as well as audience reactions, for example:

- views on how the scene establishes a conventional comedy plot in contrast with the unusual wooing of Kate by Petruchio;
- the idea of the clever, resourceful servant represented by Tranio, his relationship with Lucentio and how he controls the subplot;
- consideration of where the comedy comes from (e.g. role reversal, language) and how it could be effectively conveyed in performance.

02 *Twelfth Night*

AO2 Focus might be on:

- the significance of the scene structurally as the first meeting of Viola and Olivia;
- the visual comedy of Viola's attempts to act like a man;
- dramatic irony arising from the audience's knowledge of Viola's identity and her feelings for Orsino;
- the visual impact of Olivia's mourning dress and veil;
- Viola's use of imagery;
- Olivia's listing of Orsino's qualities;
- Olivia's use of questions;
- Olivia's sort soliloquy and the use of rhetorical questions and exclamations to show her emotional state.

AO3 Focus might be on:

- The setting in Olivia's garden and the larger setting of Illyria;
- the traditions of Twelfth Night – the natural order inverted;
- the relative social status of the characters – Viola playing a servant's role but being a 'gentleman';

- the use of boys to play women in Elizabethan theatre;
- conventions of courtship reflected in Viola's language;
- gender roles – Olivia's unusual status as a powerful woman;
- attitudes to sex, gender and sexuality changing over time.

AO4 Focus might be on:

- the importance of disguise and mistaken identity in comedy;
- the comedy of courtship and marriage – the need for true love to triumph.

AO5

You could develop any of the points made above and suggest different meanings arising from them as well as audience reactions, for example:

- Viola's love for Orsino, compared to his love for Olivia, and the effect of her 'willow cabin' speech on Olivia and on the audience;
- Shakespeare's use of disguise to explore issues about love and gender, its comic effect and possible audience reactions;
- Parallels between Olivia's and Viola's situations – both in mourning for their brothers, both falling in love, both alone and forced to be independent.

AO2/AO4: As you're reading the unseen extract, annotate or highlight the text. Look for striking examples of the writer's techniques and for points that relate to ideas about comedy and themes that are important elsewhere in the play.

03 *The Taming of the Shrew*

AO2 Focus might be on:

- the structure of the play, following courtships and ending in marriages;
- the impact of the ending when Petruchio wins his bet with the other bridegrooms;
- Katherina's final speech and the language she uses about marriage;
- the absurdity of Petruchio and Katherina's wedding and the contrast with wedding feast at the end;
- the function of Bianca and the widow.

AO3 Focus might be on:

- traditional Christian ideas about marriage;
- the practice (common in the 16th century) of marrying for financial gain or security rather than love;
- changing ideas about marriage and its importance/relevance;
- feminist ideas/interpretations and how they might influence modern productions and/or audience reactions.

AO4 Focus might be on:

- comedies ending in marriage, signifying both happiness for the characters and the restoration of the proper order;
- different types of comedy and questions about whether the ending should be taken seriously or could be considered satirical;
- the induction and whether the main action being 'a play within a play' makes a difference to audience reactions.

AO5

You might have focussed on some of the following ideas:

For the proposition	Against the proposition
The impact of the ending and Katherina's acceptance of Petruchio's authority.	Different interpretations of the ending in production.
The eloquence of her language in the final speech and its reflection of traditional ideas about marriage.	The idea that Katherina has been forced into submission and does not mean what she says.
How the play reflects Elizabethan ideas about marriage and women's roles and reinforces accepted social norms.	How the taming of Katherina might disturb audiences and cause them to question traditional ideas about marriage.
The importance of marriage being based on love; the change in Katherina and Petruchio's relationship when they fall in love.	The fact that neither Katherina nor Petruchio marries for love and doubts over whether they do fall in love.

04 *The Taming of the Shrew*

AO2 Focus might be on:

- use of disguise by Lucentio, Tranio, Hortensio and the merchant;
- use of soliloquies especially by Petruchio;
- the kiss in the street, when Petruchio and Katherina's marriage is shown to be changed;
- change in the language used by both Katherina and Petruchio;
- the dramatic impact of Katherina's submission to Petruchio at the end.

AO3 Focus might be on:

- ideas in literature about love transforming people's characters;
- religious ideas about salvation;
- differing perspectives over time about whether the transformation in Katherina is desirable.

AO4 Focus might be on:

- the role of disguise and physical transformation in comedy;
- how finding love and achieving a happy ending often depends on characters changing;
- didactic/moral aspects of comedy – characters learning from experience and developing.

AO5

You might have focussed on some of the following ideas:

For the proposition	Against the proposition
The focus on Katherina's transformation from shrew to wife and its successful achievement.	Whether the transformation has been forced on her and whether it is genuine.
How Petruchio is transformed from a rough adventurer to a loving husband.	The idea that Petruchio does not change but acts more lovingly to Katherina because he has got his way.
The implications of Lucentio's use of disguise to gain Bianca's love (disguise allows the expression of true feelings) and Petruchio's costume when he marries Katherina.	The purpose of Lucentio's disguise being simply to advance the plot and Petruchio's just to annoy Katherina and get laughs.

05 *Twelfth Night*

AO2 Focus might be on:

- the use of their scenes to contrast with more 'serious' scenes;
- comic names;
- physical comedy;
- Sir Toby's extravagant use of language;
- use of puns and bawdy language;
- contrast (possibly physical) between them.

AO3 Focus might be on:

- satire on the 'sale' of knighthoods by James I;
- Twelfth Night traditions of disorder and celebration;
- awareness of Puritan campaigns against drink and the theatre;
- their roots in 17th century England despite the play's setting in the unreal world of Illyria.

AO4 Focus might be on:

- the importance of subplots, their reflection of main plot themes and their eventual coming together with main plots;
- satirical traditions reflected in portrayal of these characters and Malvolio;
- broad, bawdy and physical comedy in the theatre.

AO5

You might have focussed on some of the following ideas:

For the proposition	Against the proposition
How their scenes are used to break up the romantic plots and provide broad comedy of a kind not seen in the main plot but that would not be missed if it were not there.	The connections between the main and subplots, for example: Sir Andrew as a suitor to Olivia; the duel between Sir Andrew and Viola; the themes of disorder.
The comic effect of Sir Toby's drunkenness, Sir Andrew's foolishness and their interactions with other characters, notably Malvolio and Viola.	How audiences may not always find their actions funny, especially the plot against Malvolio and perhaps Sir Toby's use of Sir Andrew for his own ends.
The lack of any depth or subtlety in their characters – they might be seen as stereotypes.	Audience reactions to their situations (there may be a certain amount of pathos); Sir Toby's feelings for Maria.

06 *Twelfth Night*

AO2 Focus might be on:

- melancholy mood at the beginning;
- the impact of the song at the end;
- the use of music to create mood;
- Malvolio's 'mad scene' and his exit jarring with the happy ending;
- the language and imagery used by Orsino, Olivia and Viola.

AO3 Focus might be on:

- possible tragic effects of gender confusion;
- tension between traditions like Twelfth Night and the rise of puritanism;
- attitudes to madness.

AO4 Focus might be on:

- comedies, like tragedies, showing the world turned upside down, the difference being that order is restored by marriage and not death;
- comedy, particularly satire, used to shed light on and criticise human folly and weakness;
- laughter as cathartic experience.

AO5

You might have focussed on some of the following ideas:

For the proposition	Against the proposition
The melancholia of Orsino, Olivia's self-indulgent mourning, Viola's loss of her twin and how their misplaced loves could be seen as tragic.	How Olivia, Orsino and Viola are all transformed by love and how the confusions they suffer are a source of amusement, helped by the knowledge that all will be well at the end.
The cruelty of the treatment of Malvolio, the possibility of his descent into madness and his final exit.	Malvolio's fate being entirely deserved because of his behaviour, and so being part of a satisfactory comic ending; his 'madness' providing real comedy.
How the misunderstandings of the plot bring the play close to a tragic ending that is only prevented by an improbable denouement.	How the complications of the plot increase its comedy and how true love triumphs in the end.

Your response should be 'informed by different interpretations' (AO5). There is huge body of Shakespearean criticism and you should have considered some of it. It can help to refer to critics by name or to schools of criticism.

Section C

For **AO2** the examiners are looking for the same things in both questions 7 and 8:

- the structure of the drama text;
- the use of dialogue, dramatic action, exits and entrances, and soliloquies in the drama text;
- the possible use of a poetry text or a novel and how their methods shape meaning;
- the writers' uses of structural, linguistic and other devices to shape meaning.

07

AO3 Focus might be on:

- the class-based nature of society, shown in *She Stoops to Conquer*, *The Importance of Being Earnest* and *Emma*;
- racial tensions in *Small Island*;
- Christian ideas of morality and sin in *The Nun's Priest's Tale*, 'The Flea' and 'Tam O'Shanter';
- satirical exposure of human flaws in 'A Satirical Elegy', *Emma* and *The Importance of Being Earnest*.

AO4 Focus might be on:

- portrayals of older women as monstrously snobbish yet comic in *She Stoops to Conquer*, *The Importance of Being Earnest*, *Emma* and 'My Rival's House';
- violent characters in *Small Island*, *The Nun's Priest's Tale* and 'Tam O'Shanter';
- potential villains treated comically and so seen in a different way in 'Not My Best Side', 'The Flea' and *She Stoops to Conquer*;
- protagonists acting immorally or dishonestly and so becoming potential villains in *The Importance of Being Earnest*, *Emma* and 'Tam O'Shanter'.

AO5

You might have focussed on some of the following ideas:

For the proposition	Against the proposition
Mrs Hardcastle's attempts to foil her niece's happiness and keep her fortune in *She Stoops to Conquer*; how she is comically vanquished and made to look ridiculous.	The audience's awareness that Mrs Hardcastle is never a serious threat because of Tony's willingness to help Miss Neville and the general tone of the comedy of *She Stoops to Conquer*.
Lady Bracknell's determination to preserve social distinctions despite its effect on her daughter and how she is defeated by a combination of comic plotting and outrageous revelation.	The absurdity of the comedy of *The Importance of Being Earnest* making any threat far from serious and Lady Bracknell's ending being as happy as anyone else's.
Frank Churchill's deceit and his manipulation of other characters in *Emma*; Emma's own malice towards characters such as Miss Bates and Robert Martin; Mrs Elton's attitude to others.	None of the characters in *Emma* being serious villains – Frank's actions coming from his love for Jane; any harm done by Emma also being inadvertent and she learns from her mistake; Mrs Elton being just silly.

Michael and Bernard as villains in different ways in *Small Island*; Michael being killed and Bernard humiliated.	In *Small Island*, Michael not being malicious and his death a tragedy, not a punishment; Bernard's racism being normal for men of his time and his ending being reasonably happy.
The fox as the villain of *The Nun's Priest's Tale*, killing Pertelote and almost killing Chanticleer; the fox satisfactorily defeated by Chanticleer's cleverness.	How the fox in *The Nun's Priest's Tale* survives, potentially to kill more hens.
Nannie almost catching Tam O'Shanter, putting his soul in danger, before he defeats her by cutting his horse's tail; the general of 'A Satirical Elegy' portrayed as a villain by Swift, but one who is defeated by death and by Swift's wit.	The traditional villain, the dragon, having his own voice in 'Not My Best Side'; those responsible for destroying the poster in 'Sunny Prestatyn' being neither identified nor punished; the impossibility of satisfactorily vanquishing the devil or his followers in 'Tam O'Shanter'.

08

AO3 Focus might be on:

- a general acceptance of how society is structured reflected in the upper/middle-class worlds of *She Stoops to Conquer*, *Emma* and *The Importance of Being Earnest*;
- social class in the 20th century in *A Small Island* and 'My Rival's House';
- rural/feudal setting of *The Nun's Priest's Tale*;
- Scottish working-class rural setting of 'Tam O'Shanter'.

AO4 Focus might be on:

- satire at the expense of the upper classes in *The Importance of Being Earnest* and 'A Satirical Elegy';
- Humour at the expense of those who aspire to a higher social class in *She Stoops to Conquer*, *Emma*, *A Small Island* and 'My Rival's House';
- Problems/misunderstandings created by love across social classes in *Emma*, *The Importance of Being Earnest* and *She Stoops to Conquer*.

AO5

You might have focussed on some of the following ideas:

For the proposition	Against the proposition
Differences in manners causing mistakes over social class in *She Stoops to Conquer*; dramatic irony as Marlow and Hastings treat the Hardcastles as if they were social inferiors.	The differences in manners shown in *She Stoops to Conquer* being between the old-fashioned country people and the more sophisticated London men, who are all from the same social class.
Seemingly minor differences in status being satirised and causing comic misunderstandings in *The Importance of Being Earnest*.	The fact that most characters in *The Importance of Being Earnest* are from the same class; most of the comedy coming from romantic misunderstandings.
Emma's inconsistent approach to people from other classes, on the one hand encouraging Harriet's ambitions and, on the other, ridiculing Miss Bates and Mrs Elton.	In *Emma*, Mrs Elton's comedy coming from her foolishness and materialism; the lack of any sense of a critique of the class system in *Emma*.
Hortense's aspirations to a higher social class gently mocked in *Small Island*.	Comedy arising not from difference in social class but from pretentious behaviour and mistaken ideas in *Small Island*.
Some comedy from the reactions of the peasants in *The Nun's Priest's Tale*.	The lack of any real sense of social class in *The Nun's Priest's Tale* (especially as the main characters are animals).
The affectionately comic version of working-class rural life depicted in 'Tam O'Shanter'; middle-class aspiration mocked (perhaps snobbishly) in 'My Rival's House'; upper-class grandeur mocked in 'A Satirical Elegy'.	'Tam O'Shanter' as an affectionate portrayal of a rural way of life in which social class is not a concern; the lack of any references to social differences in 'Mrs Sisyphus', 'The Flea' and 'Not My Best Side'.

AO4 asks you to 'explore connections across literary texts'. The exam board stresses that this should be done in the context of comedy. Whether you are writing about two texts (Sections A and B) or one (Section C), you need to show that you have studied and understood ideas about comedy, but you must ensure that everything you say is relevant to the text and the question.

Paper 2A

Texts and Genres: Elements of Crime Writing

For **AO1,** the examiners are looking for the same things for all questions (1–11):

- quality of argument;
- organisation of ideas;
- use of appropriate concepts and terminology;
- technical accuracy.

AO1/AO5: When examiners look at 'quality of argument' and 'organisation of ideas' they are asking whether what you have written makes sense and is convincing. A quick plan can help with this. You should make your points in a logical order, using paragraphs properly, take account of different points of view, support every point you make with evidence and come to a rational conclusion that answers the question. Your objective is to convince the examiner of your point of view.

Section A

01

AO2 Focus might be on:

- first person narrative – narrator as witness;
- opening rhetorical question;
- atmospheric description, focussing on sounds;
- flashback, indicated by use of the past perfect ('had');
- vocabulary of fear ('dreadful', 'horror');
- references to time to create tension ('suddenly', 'in an instant');
- short sentences for impact ('But I saw nothing');
- use of questions and exclamations;
- use of dialogue;
- change of tone starting with 'What can it mean?'

AO3 Focus might be on:

- setting in country house;
- context of time – night-time setting;
- exotic atmosphere, incongruous in English countryside (the cheetah, the snake, Turkish slippers);
- the British Empire (Roylott's background; reference to India).

AO4 Focus might be on:

- 'locked room' mystery – focus on the puzzle;
- relationship between the detective (Holmes) and his assistant (Watson);
- use of the assistant as narrator;
- Holmes's unusual ability and wide knowledge helping him to solve the mystery;
- the use of a trap to catch the criminal;
- private detective as protagonist;
- detailed description of the dead victim/criminal;
- crime solved and sense of justice being done but nobody brought to trial.

AO5

You may have developed any of the above points, suggesting what meanings arise from them and how readers might react, for example:

- ways in which Conan Doyle builds tension and keeps readers interested in the solution to the mystery, especially his use of Watson as narrator;
- the atmosphere of fear and evil created and the incongruity of the presence of the exotic and dangerous animals in an English country house;
- ideas about justice, the role of the detective in dispensing justice and consideration of how and why the institutions of the law are by-passed.

AO4: When you first read your unseen text, think about how it fits into the crime genre, for example: Is there a detective? Is it set at a trial? Does it focus on the victim? Does it focus on the criminal? What is the nature of the crime? Everything you write must be related to the extract as crime writing.

Section B

02 *Selected Poems* – George Crabbe, Robert Browning and Oscar Wilde

AO2 Focus might be on:

- beginnings and endings;
- use of climaxes;
- use of rhyme and rhythm;

- use of narrative verse paragraphs in 'Peter Grimes';
- dramatic monologue form in Browning;
- ballad form in Wilde;
- use of voices (personae in Browning) and narrative viewpoint;
- language and linguistic devices (patterning, imagery etc.).

AO3 Focus might be on:

- use of settings (the gaol in Wilde);
- the true story behind *The Ballad of Reading Gaol*;
- Peter Grimes's abuse of the apprentice system;
- the social status of Browning's characters;
- Browning's interest in extreme behaviour;
- power of men over women in 'My Last Duchess' and 'Porphyria's Lover';
- Wilde's interest in the experience of punishment rather than crime.

AO4 Focus might be on:

- interest in the workings of the criminal mind;
- descriptions of extreme violence;
- the power criminals have over their victims;
- the power of the law.

AO5

You might have focussed on some of the following ideas:

For the proposition	Against the proposition
Browning's use of dramatic monologues to give insight into how criminals exercise power through violence – the Duke demonstrating his power through violence; Porphyria's 'lover' using physical power to achieve his end; the woman in the laboratory enjoying the power over her rivals that poison gives her.	'My Last Duchess' and 'The Laboratory' not focussing on the violence of the crimes; the narrators of 'Porphyria's Lover' and 'The Laboratory' not so much exercising power as gaining power by their acts.
Peter Grimes's power over his apprentices, how he abuses it and his apparent enjoyment of violence.	Peter Grimes's descent into violence originating in his lack of power as a child; his motivation being unknowable.
Wilde's fascination with the details of the trooper's hanging; capital punishment as an instrument for reinforcing the power of the state.	The lack of detail Wilde gives about the trooper's violent crime or the crimes of other prisoners; capital punishment criticised as part of a flawed punitive system rather than as an instrument of power.

03 *The Rime of the Ancient Mariner*

AO2 Focus might be on:

- the narrative frame;
- beginnings and endings;
- the seven parts of the narrative;
- use of climaxes;
- use of rhyme and rhythm;
- use of voices;
- language of crime and punishment;
- linguistic devices;
- patterning;
- religious imagery.

AO3 Focus might be on:

- use of settings;
- literary/folk traditions about wandering sinners;
- Christian religious context;
- Romantic ideas about man and nature.

AO4 Focus might be on:

- the mariner's punishment and its effect on him;
- the albatross as a victim of a crime against God and/or nature;
- the other sailors as victims of his crime;
- the act seen as sin rather than crime and the distinction to be made.

AO5

You might have focussed on some of the following ideas:

For the proposition	Against the proposition
• the mariner's wandering, the never-ending nature of his punishment and the weight of his conscience.	• the mariner's punishment being just and identifying him as criminal/sinner, not victim.
• his punishment by having the albatross hung round his neck, the horror of his visions and his haunting by the 'ghostly crew'.	• the death of the albatross being entirely his doing and the deaths of the crew being the result of his original crime – the crew and the bird as victims.
• the victim of his crime being a bird not a human; the shooting of the albatross not being the cause of what happens next, the crew's reactions being based on superstition.	• the symbolic and mystical nature of the poem, what the albatross represents and the mariner's action as a crime against God, nature and humanity.

AO2: Comment in detail on the writers' use of language, making sure you choose appropriate examples form the text. Focus on how your examples relate to the question and crime genre, for example: the language of violence and suffering, imagery of redemption.

04 *When Will There Be Good News?*

AO2 Focus might be on:

- beginning and ending;
- use of climaxes relating to justice and revenge;
- use of interconnected stories;
- omniscient narrator and free indirect discourse;
- use of dialogue;
- linguistic devices;
- literary allusions;
- cyclical structure.

AO3 Focus might be on:

- use of settings;
- background of justice, punishment and the parole system;
- allusions to religion, classical myths and literature;
- gender issues and feminist slant of novel;
- 21st century relative morality, driven by emotion rather than fixed ideas of right and wrong;
- 21st century focus on victims of crime.

AO4 Focus might be on:

- the role of detectives as avengers/dispensers of justice in crime fiction;
- failure to bring criminals to justice through the legal system (common in crime fiction);
- personal, emotional involvement of detectives with victims of crime.

AO5

You might have focussed on some of the following ideas:

For the proposition	Against the proposition
The foregrounding of the murder of Jo's family and its effect on her, leading to her pursuit of revenge.	A sense that Jo, as a victim, is damaged by the crime and justified in her feelings.
Brodie's and especially Munroe's ideas about justice and their motivations for doing their jobs.	Brodie's and Munroe's roles as servants of justice, and Munroe's obligation to follow procedure whatever her personal feelings.
The death of Decker as a result of Jo's visit, despite having served his sentence; his suicide potentially damning him eternally according to his beliefs.	A sense that Decker's sentence was too light and so justice was not done and that, whatever Jo might have said or done, his suicide is his responsibility.
Brodie's collusion in Jo's killing of her kidnappers, the failure to charge her with any crime and her subsequent happy life.	The idea that her actions were self-defence and that Brodie is right not to report what he knows.
Mr Hunter being charged with arson despite it having been established that he was not responsible, and Billy apparently not being charged with anything.	The idea that Hunter is still responsible because of his involvement with the criminal gang and that Billy's crimes are minor and not the focus of the novel.

05 *Atonement*

AO2 Focus might be on:

- beginning and ending;
- use of climaxes;
- use of different timelines, related to each other;
- the postmodern ending, drawing attention to it being fiction;

- use of the (apparently) third-person narrator;
- the unreliability of the narrator in hindsight;
- use of irony;
- significance of the title.

AO3 Focus might be on:

- the setting in an upper-class country house;
- social class and the behaviour of upper-class families;
- the novel as post-modernist literature;
- the novel as a Bildungsroman;
- attitudes to women and girls at the time the novel is set;
- changing ideas about sexual crimes and feminist perspectives;
- the need to protect the respectable facade of the upper middle class.

AO4 Focus might be on:

- the setting recalling country house mysteries of the 1920s and '30s;
- subversion of the norms of the crime novel, as criminals are rewarded rather than punished, while an innocent man is punished;
- changing ideas about sexual crimes and feminist perspectives;
- uncertainty about whether Lola ever knows who raped her;
- ideas about whether legal processes can be relied on;
- ideas about what is meant by 'victims'.

AO5

You might have focussed on some of the following ideas:

For the proposition	Against the proposition
The real suffering endured by Robbie and Cecilia, ending in their deaths.	The survival of Cecilia and Robbie's love – love triumphing over adversity.
The novel as the story of a miscarriage of justice, with Robbie as the victim of a flawed system as well as of a malicious teenager and a criminal who does not tell the truth.	The idea that Robbie might be in some ways a 'victim' but he is the victim of Briony's malice, not of Paul Marshall's crime – that must be Lola.
The ambiguity of Lola's position and whether she knows the identity of her attacker and is complicit in his crime, especially as she ends up marrying him.	Discussion of whether or not Lola does know that the attacker was Paul – and of whether this makes any difference to her role as victim, perhaps seen in feminist terms.
Briony's atonement seen as self-indulgent and a rewriting of the facts in order to paint herself as a victim rather than an accessory to Marshall's crime.	The idea that Briony's life has been unfairly scarred by her crime, that she is wrong to blame herself and can, therefore, be presented as a victim of Marshall.

O6: *Oliver Twist*

AO2 Focus might be on:

- the novel's picaresque structure;
- the conventional ending, the criminals being punished;
- the use of fiction to expose social problems;
- the third-person intrusive narrator, who comments on the action;
- the language used by characters such as Bumble;
- the satirical treatment of officers of the law.

AO3 Focus might be on:

- the setting in 1830s London;
- the Poor Law Act of 1834 and the harshness of the workhouses;
- lack of trust in the police and courts common in 19th century Britain;
- the threat of severe punishment – hanging or transportation;
- Dickens's attitude to the institutions of the law as incompetent and/or corrupt;
- Differences between 19th and 21st century attitudes to crime and punishment.

AO4 Focus might be on:

- the London settings creating a background of poverty and criminality;
- scenes in court, showing how justice is or is not served;
- the inadequacy of law enforcement and how justice is only done because of middle-class amateurs seeking the truth;
- scenes set in and outside prisons;
- the tying up of loose ends when punishment and rewards are meted out at the end;
- the variety of criminal acts depicted, climaxing in murder.

AO5

You might have focussed on some of the following ideas:

For the proposition	Against the proposition
The irony of Bumble's statement given that he is a legal official and he has been shown to be cruel and corrupt.	Bumble and the guardians being used to demonstrate the inadequacies of the Poor Law in particular, rather than the law in general.
The failure of the law to protect vulnerable characters such as Agnes, Oliver and Nancy.	The sense that Dickens nowhere states or implies that the law's business is to protect the vulnerable (except in the case of the Poor Law) and that the misfortunes of Nancy are due to poverty and the actions of criminals.
The humorous portrayal of various court appearances and trials, such as Oliver's appearance before the incompetent Mr Fang and the Artful Dodger's entertaining attempt to defend himself.	How, although the scenes are comic, both these court appearances end with justice being done – Oliver being released (and helped by 'the bluff old fellow', a sympathetic legal official) and the Dodger being found guilty.
The fact that when justice is done it is not done through official channels – Fagin is caught because he is betrayed by Claypole, while Monks is caught and punished by middle-class amateurs Brownlow and Maylie, and Sykes falls to his death while being pursued.	The sense that Fagin is punished by due process of law (and deserves what he gets) and that Sykes is about to be caught by the pursuing police 'in the King's name'; a feeling on the part of some readers that Dickens might treat Monks differently because of his background.

AO3 asks you to comment on 'contexts in which literary texts are written', so you need to show that you understand the social, moral, political and literary world it was produced in – but remember that this is an examination, not a quiz. The examiners do not want to be told everything you know about, for example, life in the 1830s. Every reference you make to context must arise naturally from the point you are making in response to the question.

07 *Brighton Rock*

AO2 Focus might be on:

- beginning and ending;
- use of climaxes, relating to questions of right and wrong/good and evil;
- the third-person narrative – detached yet omniscient;
- shifting focus between characters, especially Ida and Pinkie;
- use of religious language and terminology;
- descriptive language.

AO3 Focus might be on:

- the setting in 1930s Brighton, its superficial glamour and materialism;
- the criminal underworld, the world of the racecourse and gang warfare;
- the poverty of Rose's and Pinkie's deprived backgrounds;
- the importance of Catholic beliefs and traditions, giving Pinkie and Rose their concepts of good and evil;
- ideas of heaven and hell;
- links to medieval morality plays;
- the more secular 20th century world that Ida moves in;
- the moral, didactic aspect of the novel.

AO4 Focus might be on:

- the role of Ida as amateur detective, and, by implication, arbiter of right and wrong;
- interest in the psychology of the criminal;
- the ending with Pinkie punished (possibly eternally) and Rose saved;
- interest in the nature (and existence) of evil.

AO5

You might have focussed on some of the following ideas:

For the proposition	Against the proposition
How, despite Greene overtly making the distinction, he does not explain what he means by it apart from that in Rose's mind good and evil are 'stronger foods' than 'right and wrong', suggesting the difference is merely a question of how strongly one feels about morality.	The reference to 'stronger foods' suggesting that, for believers, 'good and evil' are larger, more fundamental ideas than 'right and wrong', inextricably linked to belief in God and ideas of eternal salvation or damnation.
How 'wrong' and 'evil' are just two different words used to describe the same actions – Ida pursues Pinky because she knows that what he has done is wrong, while Pinky and Rose are aware that his deeds are evil, and they all know that he deserves to be punished.	How marriage outside the Church concerns Pinky and Rose at least as much as murder, their sense of good and evil being based on whether they obey the teachings of the Church, whereas Ida's ideas of right and wrong are connected more with legality and secular ideas of proper behaviour.

How both concepts are based on Judeo-Christian theology – while Pinky and Rose are conscious of this because of their Catholic background and use more religious terminology, Rose too refers to the Bible when she speaks of 'an eye for an eye'.	How Ida does not link 'an eye for an eye' to religion, using it simply as a common expression and her 'spiritual authority' is the Ouija board.

08 *The Murder of Roger Ackroyd*

AO2 Focus might be on:

- beginning and ending;
- new revelations in each chapter, building up to the final revelation;
- the set piece when Poirot reveals the characters' crimes;
- use of the unreliable narrator;
- the discovery of clues throughout the novel;
- the role of Poirot the cool, logical outsider who solves the puzzle;
- use of straightforward language.

AO3 Focus might be on:

- the setting in 1920s small town in rural England, apparently settled and peaceful;
- the increasing popularity of detective stories at the time;
- readers' attempts to deduce solution as part of the genre's entertainment value;
- the country house, a typical setting for a 'locked door' mystery;
- middle-class, apparently respectable society, with its manners and rituals (mah jong, dressing for dinner etc);
- the use of characters such as Caroline, who themselves try to solve the crime.

AO4 Focus might be on:

- the private detective who is a regular in the author's novels and will be expected to solve the crime;
- readers' attempts to deduce the solution as part of the genre's entertainment value;
- Sheppard's apparent role as Poirot's assistant (replacing Hastings) and narrator in the manner of Dr Watson, used to trick the reader.

AO5

You might have focussed on some of the following ideas:

For the proposition	Against the proposition
The lack of depth and complexity in the characters, most of whom are 'types' that are expected in detective novels of the period and whose thoughts and emotions are not explored.	The necessity in the genre of not giving readers insight into the characters minds but how, nevertheless, Christie's characters do reveal feelings and motivations that can elicit sympathy from readers, for example: Miss Russell's relationship with her son; Ursula's feelings for Ralph; Major Blunt's feelings for Flora.
The role of the detective, his superior intellect, readers' trust in him to solve the mystery and the distancing of his character by using an assistant who is not entirely in his confidence.	Poirot's interest in the psychology of murder and in achieving justice, as well as his humanity shown in his compassion for the characters (including his desire to spare Caroline pain).
The importance of the final revelation, Poirot's explanation, and the 'trick' played on readers by the author.	How the ending reveals not just the identity of the murderer but his and others' feelings, giving a sense of the effect of murder on those involved, not least on the victims, Mrs Ferrars and Roger Ackroyd.

09 *Hamlet*

AO2 Focus might be on:

- beginning and ending;
- use of climaxes relating to Claudius's actions and Hamlet's response;
- the appearance of the ghost;
- Hamlet's soliloquies;
- Claudius's soliloquy;
- the play within a play;
- language and imagery.

AO3 Focus might be on:

- the divine right of kings;
- religious beliefs about judgement and damnation;
- the revenge tragedy genre;
- biblical prohibition of taking one's brother's wife;
- the society of the court;
- ideas of what might or might not be considered a crime in the 17th century.

AO4 Focus might be on:

- the cycle of violence and multiple murders;
- the trap set by Hamlet in the play within a play as a classic way of catching a criminal;
- the exploration of the criminal's guilt and motives explored in his soliloquy ('O my offence is rank').

AO5

You might have focussed on some of the following ideas:

For the proposition	Against the proposition
The enormity of the crime of killing Hamlet's father, a 'foul murder' that is not just murder but both fratricide and regicide, and the importance of the idea of the divine right of kings.	A more mundane interpretation of Claudius's crimes and his own version of his motivation – 'my crown, mine own ambition, and my queen'.
The crime of marrying his brother's wife, seen as incest, which places sexual deviance and corruption at the heart of the court.	Definitions of 'crime' – although forbidden in the Bible, kings (such as Henry VIII) did marry their brothers' widows; there is no real sense of the 'incest' having any harmful effects on anyone except Hamlet.
The ripple effect of these crimes, related to the genre of revenge tragedy, causing the deaths of Polonius, Ophelia, Rosencrantz and Guildenstern, Gertrude, Laertes, Hamlet and Claudius himself.	Claudius's crimes not in themselves being the cause of the other deaths – the court appears stable until Hamlet is urged by the ghost to seek revenge.
The idea that the crimes/sins of a king infect the whole state and makes it ungovernable, chaos in Denmark here allowing Norway to invade.	The lack of a real sense of the country suffering or Claudius being a bad king (unlike in *Macbeth* for example).

AO3 asks you to comment on 'contexts in which literary texts are […] received', which is related to AO5's 'different interpretations'. You need to be aware of how responses to a text may have changed over time and how individuals' responses may have been shaped by their society – but don't assume that everybody at any given time or in any given place shares the same ideas and values. Such assumptions are as dangerous in literary criticism as they are in life.

Section C

10

AO2 Focus might be on:

- the text's form of drama, poetry or prose;
- the use of narrators – intrusive narrator in *Oliver Twist*, unreliable narrator in *The Murder of Roger Ackroyd*;
- the use of exposition and scene setting to establish ideas of 'normal life';
- the use of resolutions to re-establish order – *Hamlet*, *Oliver Twist*, *When Will There Be Good News?*;
- the use of descriptions of settings;
- the use of religious language and imagery in *Peter Grimes*, *The Ancient Mariner*, *Brighton Rock*, *Oliver Twist*, *The Ballad of Reading Gaol* and *Hamlet*.

AO3 Focus might be on:

- settings – the ordered life of the village in *The Murder of Roger Ackroyd*, the court in *Hamlet*, the country house in *Atonement*, rural setting of *Peter Grimes*;
- social – contrast between the criminal underworld and middle-class comfort in *Oliver Twist* and *When Will There Be Good News?*;
- moral – morality based on Christian teachings in *Hamlet*, *The Ballad of Reading Gaol*, *Brighton Rock* and *Peter Grimes*; the moral relativism of *When Will There Be Good News?*; the lack of a moral sense in Browning's characters;
- historical – different ideas about what makes an ordered and stable society across time.

AO4 Focus might be on:

- comfortable lives disrupted by crime – *Atonement*, *The Murder of Roger Ackroyd*, *When Will There Be Good News?*;
- disorder created by the breaking of God's laws – *Hamlet*, *The Rime of the Ancient Mariner*, 'Peter Grimes';
- texts where the truth is not revealed to all – *Atonement*, *When Will There Be Good News?*;
- texts where justice is not done through the law – *Atonement*, *Brighton Rock*, *Oliver Twist*, *The Murder of Roger Ackroyd*;
- deaths of criminals – *The Murder of Roger Ackroyd*, *When Will There Be Good News?*, *Brighton Rock*, 'Peter Grimes', *Oliver Twist*, *Hamlet*;
- crimes unpunished – *When Will There Be Good News?*, *Atonement*, Browning's dramatic monologues.

AO5

You might have developed any of the above points, suggesting what meanings arise from those ideas and how readers might react, for example:

- Browning, Crabbe and Wilde – the Duke's preservation of his own order and desire for another wife in 'My Last Duchess'; the crimes of Peter Grimes as an aberration in the peaceful normality of rural England.
- Coleridge – normal life seen in the framing story of the wedding guest, which emphasises the abnormality of the mariner's tale; a sense of the proper spiritual and moral order being restored; justice done.

- Atkinson – cyclical structure; the murder of Jo's family as 'unfinished business', which is finished in the novel; the emphasis on the comfort and normality of middle-class life at the end, and how it is achieved by not telling the truth or doing justice; the view that justice has been done though not in a conventional way.
- McEwan – the importance to the upper-middle-class characters of their comfortable 'normal life' and the shock of it being shattered by crime; Briony's retention of a comfortable lifestyle despite (or because of) getting away with her crime; the injustice done to Robbie.
- Dickens – sense that Oliver is restored to his rightful place; the deal made with Monks and how he is not brought to justice in a conventional way although others are.
- Greene – Rose being saved and returned to a normal life; Ida returning to her humdrum normality and peace coming to Brighton; the disturbing ending suggesting that normality has not been restored.
- Christie – restoration of peaceful life in King's Abbot; Poirot's collusion in the keeping of secrets; the murderer not brought to trial to avoid scandal.
- Shakespeare – conventional restoration of order at the end, but not a return to the past.

11

AO2 Focus might be on:
- the text's form of drama, poetry or prose;
- the use of narrators – the use of structural features to draw attention to ideas about punishment;
- the use of dialogue.

AO3 Focus might be on:
- settings – prisons in *Oliver Twist* and *The Ballad of Reading Gaol*;
- historical – changing ideas about punishment, from the severe punishments of *Oliver Twist* through the acceptance of capital punishment for murder in the early 20th century to parole of 21st century;
- social – middle- and upper-class characters avoiding proper legal punishments;
- moral – questioning of the morality of some punishments in *Oliver Twist* and *The Ballad of Reading Gaol*;
- religious – ideas about the Last Judgement and the punishment of sin after death.

AO4 Focus might be on:
- capital punishment – *Oliver Twist*, *The Ballad of Reading Gaol*;
- crimes unpunished – *Atonement*, *When Will There Be Good News?*, Browning;
- crimes punished without legal process – *Oliver Twist*, *The Murder of Roger Ackroyd*, *When Will There Be Good News?*, *Brighton Rock*, *Hamlet*;
- unjust punishment – *Atonement*, 'My Last Duchess', *Oliver Twist*;
- excessive punishment – *The Ballad of Reading Gaol*, *Oliver Twist*;
- punishment by conscience or God – *Brighton Rock*, *The Rime of the Ancient Mariner*, 'Peter Grimes'.

AO5

You might have developed any of the above points, suggesting what meanings arise from those ideas and how readers might react, for example:
- Browning, Crabbe and Wilde – Wilde's focus on punishment and its effects on the punished; Wilde's graphic account of capital punishment; Browning's criminals possibly going unpunished and punishment not being his concern; Peter Grimes's self-punishment.
- Coleridge – the mariner's extreme physical and psychological punishment for killing the albatross; how the punishment extends to his innocent shipmates; how he is plagued by conscience.
- Atkinson – Decker's punishment seen as inadequate; Jo's 'punishment' of him excessive and brutal; her killing of the kidnappers as punishment rather than self-defence; the lack of punishment of her for anything she has done.
- McEwan – the unjust punishment of Robbie for the rape; the failure to punish Paul Marshall or Briony; Briony's punishment by conscience.
- Dickens – constant reminders of the harshness of 19th century punishment; punishment in the workhouse; Fagin and the Dodger punished by law while Monks is 'punished' by Brownlow and Maylie; Sikes plagued by his conscience and effectively punished by death.
- Greene – failure of the police to catch and punish criminals; gang members punishment of those who betray them; Pinkie effectively punished by death; ideas of eternal punishment.
- Christie – Sheppard 'punished' by suicide but avoiding trial; awareness of capital punishment; other characters unpunished for their minor crimes.
- Shakespeare – Hamlet's mission to punish Claudius; Laertes's desire to punish Hamlet; the relationship between punishment and revenge.

Paper 2A is an 'open book' exam, meaning you will have your set texts with you. You are expected to quote accurately. You should be able to find quotations you haven't memorised easily by now. If you can't find one quickly, however, don't let yourself get bogged down in the search. Paraphrase or use a different quotation.

Paper 2B

Texts and Genres: Elements of Political and Social Protest

For **AO1,** the examiners are looking for the same things for all questions (1–11):

- quality of argument;
- organisation of ideas;
- use of appropriate concepts and terminology;
- technical accuracy.

AO1: When examiners look at 'quality of argument' and organisation of ideas' they are asking whether what you have written makes sense and is convincing. A quick plan can help with this. You should make your points in a logical order, using paragraphs properly, take account of different points of view, support every point you make with evidence and come to a rational conclusion that answers the question. Your objective is to convince the examiner of your point of view.

Section A

01

AO2 Focus might be on:

- significance of the title;
- the impersonal voice (no involvement of the poet);
- use of the first-person plural at the beginning and end;
- the opening exclamation;
- exclamations and rhetorical questions;
- personification of Reason;
- imagery of nature;
- use of lists;
- past tense;
- regularity of iambic pentameter.

AO3 Focus might be on:

- historical context of the French Revolution and its aftermath;
- the Romantic movement;
- ideas about the Enlightenment and progress;
- the lack of democracy and freedom in Britain and most of the world at the time.

AO4 Focus might be on:

- expression of hope and optimism;
- ideas about common purpose;
- idealism about and belief in the goodness of mankind (ironic in view of later events).

AO5

You may have developed any of the above points, suggesting what meanings arise from them and how readers might react, for example:

- how Wordsworth's title alerts us to the 'enthusiasts' being naïve and doomed to disappointment, making the ideas expressed in the poem seem sadly deluded and unreal;
- the poem as an expression of hope and optimism, recapturing genuine feelings among many that the world could and would change, and focussing on the positive rather than dwelling on negative aspects either of the revolution or the regime it overthrew;
- ideas about the essential goodness of humanity, the unity of reason and emotion, the relationship between man and nature.

AO4: When you first read your unseen text, think about how it fits into the political and social protest genre, for example: who is protesting, someone in the text or the writer? What is he/she protesting about? Does it focus on the oppressed or dispossessed? If so, who are they? Where is it set? Everything you write must be related to the extract as writing of political or social protest.

Section B

02 *Songs of Innocence and Experience*

AO2 Focus might be on:

- the patterning and mirroring of *Innocence* and *Experience* poems;
- lyric and narrative verse;
- the structure of individual poems and relative complexity of form in *Experience*;
- range of rhyme schemes, metrical patterns etc.;
- use of contrast;
- use of rhyme and rhythm;
- use of repetition;

- use of voices;
- apparent simplicity of language;
- religious symbolism;
- imagery of oppression, imprisonment and violence.

AO3 Focus might be on:

- the use of settings (rural and urban; institutional);
- idealisation of children and childhood;
- historical context – French Revolution, Industrial Revolution;
- Romantic ideas about man and nature;
- Romantic poets' desire to break with the rules and conventions of classical poetry in order to achieve truth;
- religious context – Blake's version of Christianity and his opposition to the established church;
- ideas about education and treatment of children;
- ideas about sexual freedom.

AO4 Focus might be on:

- the presentation of protest through the idea of contrasting states;
- concern with issues such as education, child labour and slavery;
- the depiction of organised religion as oppressive and corrupting;
- belief in freedom of the body and the spirit.

AO5

You might have focussed on some of the following ideas:

For the proposition	Against the proposition
The church specifically referred to as an instrument of oppression and repression in 'The Garden of Love', 'The Little Vagabond' and 'London' in contrast to what God and religion should mean; the association of state and church criticised in 'The Little Vagabond' ('God & his Priest & King') and implied criticism of the state in 'Holy Thursday' (Experience), 'The Little Black Boy', 'The Chimney Sweeper' (Experience) and 'London'.	Oppression as a result of man's fallen state or simply experience, shown not through rules and institutions but also through personal relationships, as in 'The Clod & The Pebble', 'Nurse's Song' (Experience), 'My Pretty Rose Tree' and 'A Poison Tree'.
Formal education and institutional charity seen as oppressive in 'The School Boy' and 'Holy Thursday' (Experience).	A more positive side of institutional charity shown in 'Holy Thursday' (Experience).
The idea that the divine spirit exists in humans and flourishes when unfettered by institutions and rules expressed in *Songs of Innocence*, for example: 'The Little Black Boy', 'The Lamb', 'The Echoing Green', 'The Divine Image'.	The idea that the *Songs of Innocence* and the *Songs of Experience* are complementary; the idea that the *Innocence* poems can be read as ironic, expressing a naïve, incomplete view of the world, for example in 'Holy Thursday', 'Nurse's Song', 'The Chimney Sweeper' and 'Laughing Song'.

03 *Selected Poems* (Harrison)

AO2 Focus might be on:

- circular structure of 'V';
- range of forms – free verse, elegiac verse ('V'), lyrical verse, sonnet form ('Working');
- first person and other voices;
- contrast in language – Standard English, Greek, colloquial and vulgar/obscene language;
- imagery and symbolism;
- use of repetition;
- use of different voices.

AO3 Focus might be on:

- political and social context of 1980s Britain;
- the poet's grammar school and university education in 1940s/50s;
- personal experience of effects of success;
- classical, English and other literature;
- Gray's *Elegy* and its influence on 'V';
- Pre-20th century industrial history.

AO4 Focus might be on:

- the experience of the lower/working classes;
- idea of giving a voice to the voiceless;
- the use of language to break conventions and possibly shock readers/audiences;
- awareness of the writer's role in social/political protest writing.

AO5

You might have focussed on some of the following ideas:

For the proposition	Against the proposition
The poet's own consciousness of how his education and success have separated him from his roots ('V', 'Marked with D').	His awareness of his separation from his roots making him more sympathetic to those who have not had the same opportunities.
Vivid depictions of the young unemployed involving only imagined not real interactions ('Divisions', 'V').	How his sensitive ear for overheard speech allows him to depict the disenfranchised as they really are.
The language and references in his poetry (and perhaps the mere fact of it being poetry) making it difficult for anyone but the educated to access.	How his awareness of his own familiarity with the classics and western culture gives rise to irony and self-deprecation.
The disenfranchised depicted in his poems being distant and exotic to his readers, emphasised by the language given to them, whether the Cornish of 'National Trust' or the obscenity-laden Yorkshire of 'V' (thrilling perhaps to the arty middle classes but of little interest to unemployed youths).	How he gives authentic voices to those who rarely feature in poetry, whether the working people of the 19th century or the unemployed of the 20th, and how this might change perceptions and attitudes of his readers.

AO2: Comment in detail on the writers' use of language, making sure you choose appropriate examples form the text. Focus on how your examples relate to the question and to writing of social and political, for example: the language of violence and punishment, religious and spiritual imagery.

04 *The Kite Runner*

AO2 Focus might be on:

- the novel as a Bildungsroman, tracing the narrator's development;
- use of time shifts;
- changes in setting;
- use of voices, especially after Amir's return to Afghanistan;
- the first-person narrator's perspective (from the ruling class and ethnic group);
- descriptions of Afghanistan before and after revolution.

AO3 Focus might be on:

- divisions between Pashtuns and Hazaras and their different experience;
- the effect of Amir's experience in America on his viewpoint;
- the history of Afghanistan;
- Afghan culture and traditions among emigres in America.

AO4 Focus might be on:

- Bildungsroman showing growing awareness of issues and the difference between child and adult viewpoints;
- the narrator having experience of different societies and being set up as someone (a writer) who observes and criticises;
- the use of real historical and political events;
- the effect of political and historical events on individuals.

AO5

You might have focussed on some of the following ideas:

For the proposition	Against the proposition
The nostalgic view of Amir's childhood in Kabul, especially descriptions of his home and memories of his friendship with Hassan.	His awareness, as an adult, of the inequality in the Afghanistan of his childhood and the stories of Hassan's rape and Hassan's mother's experience.
His personal experience of escape from Kabul and his family's life as immigrants in America.	The security of his life in America and his awareness that his fellow Afghans are nostalgic for a life of privilege.
The society he encounters on his return to Afghanistan and the dangerous situations he encounters.	Farid's observation that life is no different for most people; the feeling of some readers that his adventures in Kabul are melodramatic and unconvincing.

05 *Harvest*

AO2 Focus might be on:

- the historical novel used to explore present days concerns;
- short time span showing rapid change;
- use of analepsis (flashback);
- use of first-person narrator – position as outsider;
- other voices;
- biblical language;

- language that is not contemporary but not archaic either;
- use of the present tense – immediacy.

AO3 Focus might be on:

- setting in an imprecise non-industrial past;
- idea of England;
- play on ideas about rural idylls and biblical ideas of Eden before the fall;
- context of present day tensions between nationalism and internationalism/globalisation;
- the historical reality of enclosures.

AO4 Focus might be on:

- emphasis on the harm done by capitalism;
- use of, and rejection of, nostalgia, showing the harshness of life in the past;
- problems but not answers presented;
- the effect of political and historical events on individuals.

AO5

You might have focussed on some of the following ideas:

For the proposition	Against the proposition
The essentially feudal and backward nature of the village and the laissez faire attitude of Kent.	The peacefulness and harmony of the villagers' day-to-day existence, as seen by Walter.
The prejudice, mob mentality and violence shown by the villagers in their reaction to the strangers.	The strangers' responsibility for disrupting life in the village and Mistress Beldame's malevolent actions.
The ruthlessness with which Jordan acts to effect change and his motives for wanting change.	Jordan's changes seen as inevitable and, if not entirely desirable, necessary for progress.
The villagers' failure to either resist or embrace change.	The villagers' belief that the status quo is desirable but acceptance that it is not possible; their eventual acceptance of change by leaving the village.

06 *Hard Times*

AO2 Focus might be on:

- changes of scene and contrasts between scenes;
- beginning and ending;
- the three-part structure;
- the intrusive narrator;
- detailed descriptions;
- use of rhetorical and hyperbolic language;
- use of dialogue;

AO3 Focus might be on:

- setting in industrial Lancashire;
- the consequences of the Poor Law of 1834;
- the centrality of Christianity in Victorian life;
- child labour;
- Victorian attitudes to women and children;
- Dickens's reputation as a campaigner on social issues;
- the practice of publishing novels in parts in popular magazines;
- the rise of organised labour.

AO4 Focus might be on:

- the tendency for literature of social and political process to present extremes and see issues in black and white terms;
- sympathy for the oppressed, often slipping into sentimentality;
- the effects of industrialisation and capitalism on individuals;

AO5

You might have focussed on some of the following ideas:

For the proposition	Against the proposition
The stereotypical presentation of working-class communities (both the mill hands and the circus people) as friendly and supportive despite their poverty.	The way in which the union members turn on Stephen and send him to Coventry; the ambition of Bounderby and Bitzer.
The one-dimensional portraits of Stephen and Rachael, their apparent lack of understanding of the issues that affect them and their uncomplicated feelings.	The strength of Rachael and Stephen's feelings for each other.

The stereotypical and unconvincing version of their speech.	The immediacy and roughness of their dialogue as conveyed by Dickens.
Their sentimental version of religion, e.g. Rachael referring to her dead sister as an 'angel'.	Rachael and Stephen's moral probity and Rachael's compassion for Stephen's wife.
The appeal of compliant and attractive working-class women like Sissy and Rachael to middle-class characters and possibly readers.	The complexity of Sissy's reaction to her situation, cooperating with the Gradgrinds but retaining her integrity and spontaneity; Rachael and Sissy shown to be superior to the middle-class women (and men).

AO3 asks you to comment on 'contexts in which literary texts are written', so you need to show that you understand the social, moral, political and literary world it was produced in – but remember that this is an examination, not a quiz. The examiners do not want to be told everything you know about, for example, life in the 1840s. Every reference you make to context must arise naturally from the point you are making in response to the question.

07 *Henry IV Part 1*

AO2 Focus might be on:

- the opening showing England suffering the effects of his deposition of Richard II;
- plot tracing the pursuit of power by Hotspur, Worcester and others;
- contrast between Henry's statesman-like language and Hotspur's violent, immoderate language;
- imagery of, for example, violent weather, bloodshed;
- Falstaff/Hal subplot comically mirroring rebellion;
- use of different settings;
- visual power of battle scenes.

AO3 Focus might be on:

- belief in the divine right of kings;
- questions over the legitimacy of Henry's claim to the throne and the Tudor version of history;
- the background of the events of *Richard II*;
- the power of the noble families;
- father/son relationships.

AO4 Focus might be on:

- instability of the state and the unknown potential results of rebellion;
- the text seen as supporting the status quo and the restoration of it at the end, whatever the rights and wrongs of Henry's claim.

AO5 You might have focussed on some of the following ideas:

For the proposition	Against the proposition
The appeal of Hotspur as a character – his bravery, his volatility, his love for his wife and his unconventionality; passion and poetry of Glendower.	Hotspur as a selfish, unreliable and dangerous character; Glendower as superstitious and unreliable; Worcester as devious; Northumberland as cowardly and dull.
The humour and wit of Hal's subplot and his outgoing, spontaneous character as a contrast to his careful, diplomatic father.	Hal as irresponsible and immature; his rebellion only appealing as long as it does not threaten the stability of the state.
The appeal of the underdog, sympathy for the causes of the rebels and the excitement of the battles.	The rebels' motives – pride, greed and desire for power – and their disunity and ineffectiveness.

08 *A Doll's House*

AO2 Focus might be on:

- three-act structure;
- unity of time, space and action;
- setting the same throughout – domestic, middle-class, respectable;
- time – three days over Christmas;
- use of voices/dialogue;
- manners of the time and class reflected in dialogue.

AO3 Focus might be on:

- 19th century middle-class Norway;
- the importance of money/financial issues;
- gender roles;
- influence of 19th century feminist movements;
- the mixed reaction to the play on first performance;
- differences in audience assumptions then and now.

AO4 Focus might be on:
- the importance of conventional behaviour and outward appearances to the middle classes;
- the focus on the effects of a society's norms on the identity of the individual;
- the role of women in the 19th century and expectations of their behaviour.

AO5

You might have focussed on some of the following ideas:

For the proposition	Against the proposition
The relationship between Nora and Helmer, their childish language, her yearning for treats and her complaints to other characters.	Nora's infantilisation at the hands of her husband and father being a result of living in a patriarchal society.
The comfort of her situation compared to others (Mrs Linde, Krogstad, Dr Rank, the maids) and the support she has had from her husband and father.	Her apparently happy and successful marriage as an illusion; her conviction that she has sacrificed herself to help her husband and father.
Her emphasis on her own feelings, and her desire to be independent and discover herself as an individual.	Her individuality having been denied because of her gender and class.
Her lack of concern of the consequences of her action for others, especially her children.	Her former concern for others having held her back and being a symptom of the patriarchal society she lives in.

09 *The Handmaid's Tale*

AO2 Focus might be on:

- dystopian form;
- first-person narrative;
- fictional diary/autobiography;
- academic commentary in last chapter;
- chronology including flashbacks and time jumps;
- awareness of process of memory and reconstruction;
- biblical language and imagery;
- use of colour symbolism;
- euphemism and gendered language.

AO3 Focus might be on:

- Christian/biblical context;
- links with American history: Puritan society of 17th century and slavery;
- parallels with Iran, Afghanistan, Romania;
- awareness of 1970s/80s feminism;
- awareness of the 'religious right' in late 20th century America;
- 21st century concerns about issues of identity politics, free speech and the tensions between them;
- ideas about patriarchal structures.

AO4 Focus might be on:

- ideas of what is a feminist work of literature (see Atwood's introduction);
- the use of the first-person narrator giving voice to the oppressed;
- the novel's focus on the experience of women;
- relevance of the novel to various forms of oppression and various societies.

AO5

You might have focussed on some of the following ideas:

For the proposition	Against the proposition
The ways in which the state oppresses and persecutes men as well as women, vividly demonstrated by the hanging bodies on the wall and shown in the fates of Luke, Nick and the Commander.	Women shown consistently as being controlled by men and specifically controlled because of their gender.
Atwood's implied critique of 20th century feminist movements, especially campaigns against pornography and for reproductive choice, summed up in Offred's references to a 'women's culture' being achieved in Gilead.	The question of what is meant by feminism – there are (and have been over time) many different interpretations of the term, the debate over issues such as freedom of expression continuing today.
The subtlety and complexity of Atwood's presentation of relationships between men and women, especially Offred's relationships with Luke, the Commander and Nick.	The idea that the men are in control in all these relationships and that they could be using Offred's sexuality to control her.
The role and complicity of women in Gilead's power structure – the Aunts, the Wives, the Salvaging, betrayals.	The women who cooperate with the state as traitors to their sex and/or unknowing victims of patriarchy.

AO3 asks you to comment on 'contexts in which literary texts are [...] received', which is related to AO5's 'different interpretations'. You need to be aware of how responses to a text may have changed over time and how individuals' responses may have been shaped by their society – but don't assume that everybody at any given time or in any given place shares the same ideas and values. Such assumptions are as dangerous in literary criticism as they are in life.

Section C

10

AO2 Focus might be on:

- the text's form of drama, poetry or prose;
- use of narrators – first-person narrators in *The Handmaid's Tale*, *Harvest* and *The Kite Runner*; intrusive narrator in *Hard Times*;
- structure – use of time shifts and the pseudo-academic paper in *The Handmaid's Tale*; the parallel subplot of Hal's 'rebellion' in *Henry IV Part 1*;
- language of oppression and rebellion in *Harvest*, *The Handmaid's Tale* and *Songs of Innocence and Experience*;
- imagery.

AO3 Focus might be on:

- settings (time and place) – 20th century Afghanistan in *The Kite Runner*; 19th century industrial Britain in *Hard Times*;
- social – the feudal village in *Harvest*; contrast between middle-class and working-class life in *Hard Times*;
- moral – Blake's representation of child labour, slavery etc.; the Taliban's treatment of children in *The Kite Runner*;
- historical – feminist movements of the 19th and 20th centuries (*A Doll's House*, *The Handmaid's Tale*); the Poor Law and industrialisation (*Hard Times*); kingship and rebellion in medieval England (*Henry IV Part 1*);
- use of imagined societies – *The Handmaid's Tale*, *Harvest*.

AO4 Focus might be on:

- protests and rebellions crushed by the state – *The Kite Runner*, *The Handmaid's Tale*, *Henry IV Part 1*;
- revolutions that turn to tyranny – *The Kite Runner*, *The Handmaid's Tale*;
- individuality crushed – *Songs of Innocence and Experience*, *Hard Times*, *The Handmaid's Tale*;
- ineffective protest – *Harvest*, *Hard Times*, Harrison;
- endings where the outcome is uncertain – *A Doll's House*, *The Handmaid's Tale*;
- outcomes seen in context of historical change – *Songs of Innocence and Experience*, *A Doll's House*, *Hard Times*, *The Kite Runner*.

AO5

You might have developed any of the above points, suggesting what meanings arise from those ideas and how readers might react, for example:

- Blake – strong sense of rebellion and protest in *Songs of Experience*, especially in poems dealing with social issues, without a sense of success or failure within the poems; readers' awareness that society has changed along the lines desired by Blake.
- Harrison – the poet's instinct for rebellion contrasted with the comfort of his 'establishment' life; sense of pointless rebellion, for example by 'skins'.
- Hosseini – the first revolution having little or no impact on Afghan lives but allowing the Russian invasion and subsequent Taliban revolution, leading to greater oppression; the Taliban's revolution being successful on its own terms.
- Crace – the lack of any organised or coordinated protest apart from when the women are arrested; the ease with which Jordan defeats the villagers when they do protest; a sense of the inevitability of change and the futility of resistance.
- Dickens – the negative attitude to the Union and Dickens's failure to tell us whether it has any effect; the tragic consequences for Stephen Blackpool of standing up for himself; the changes in Gradgrind and his attitudes resulting from Louisa's rebellion.
- Atwood – the success of the revolution in establishing Gilead; the apparent failure of feminism pre-Gilead and the irony of the revolution having achieved some of Offred's mother's aims; the constant failures of rebels against Gilead; revelations about what happened later in the academic paper; uncertainty about Offred's fate.
- Ibsen – Nora's failure to change Helmer and their relationship; the sense that the odds are stacked against her; her success in finally asserting her individuality; uncertainty about how her rebellion will end.
- Shakespeare – the failure of Hotspur's rebellion; reasons for its failure; the importance of stability and the strengthening of Henry's power; the audience's awareness that Henry has gained power by rebellion so the play could be proof that rebellion can end in success.

11

AO2 Focus might be on:

- the text's form of drama, poetry or prose;
- use of narrators – intrusive narrator in *Hard Times*, first-person narrators in *The Handmaid's Tale* and the *Kite Runner*;
- use of academic voice in *A Handmaid's Tale*;
- time shifts/flashbacks in *The Kite Runner*, *Harvest* and *A Handmaid's Tale*;
- use of contrast – *Songs of Innocence and Experience*, *Hard Times*;
- structure – dramatic structure and endings of *Henry IV Part 1* and *A Doll's House*;
- dialogue – contrast in Hotspur's and Henry's language in *Henry IV Part 1*, language used to each other by Helmer and Nora in *A Doll's House*;

AO3 Focus might be on:

- settings (time and place) – factory and school in *Hard Times*; Afghanistan/America in *The Kite Runner*;
- social – the feudal village in *Harvest*; social stratification in *A Handmaid's Tale*; differences between the classes in *Hard Times*;
- moral – moral choices in *The Kite Runner*, *Hard Times*, *Harvest* and *A Handmaid's Tale*;
- historical – awareness of real events/movements and in *Henry IV Part 1*, *The Kite Runner*, *The Handmaid's Tale*, *A Doll's House* and *Hard Times*.

AO4 Focus might be on:

- presentation of class issues – *Hard Times*, *Harvest*, *The Kite Runner*, Harrison;
- presentation of gender issues – *A Doll's House*, *The Handmaid's Tale*, *The Kite Runner*;
- presentation of ethnic issues – *Harvest*, *The Kite Runner*;
- presentation of moral/spiritual issues – *Songs of Innocence and Experience*, *The Handmaid's Tale*, *Henry IV Part 1*, *The Kite Runner*;
- presentation of political issues – *Henry IV Part 1*, *The Kite Runner*, *The Handmaid's Tale*;
- failed solutions shown – *The Handmaid's Tale*, *The Kite Runner*;
- partial/possible solutions suggested – *Hard Times*, the *Handmaid's Tale*, *A Doll's House*, *Songs of Innocence and Experience*;

AO5

You might have developed any of the above points, suggesting what meanings arise from those ideas and how readers might react, for example:

- Blake – vivid presentation of social and spiritual oppression; whether life as portrayed in *Innocence* suggests solutions; lack of practical solutions to problems; belief in essential goodness/divinity of humanity and appeals to that spirit.
- Harrison – passionate concern with the 'voiceless' and desire to give them a voice through poetry; awareness that this achieves little; some sense that problems of poverty and disenfranchisement have been solved over time; power of education to change lives/ambiguous attitude to it.
- Hosseini – the narrator as an observer and recorder, a writer and not a politician or campaigner; awareness of problems in pre- and post-revolution Afghanistan; sense of nostalgia for old Afghanistan; personal solution to Sohrab's problem, which is impossible on a big scale and unconvincing in its execution.
- Crace – problems of progress and isolationism/ prejudice presented; attempts to solve the problems within the narrative are doomed to failure; ending with the characters all moving on but with no real sense of what will happen to them.
- Dickens – vivid but sentimental depiction of poverty; consciousness of the problems caused by industrialisation; unsympathetic portrayal of Union but no presentation of an alternative way of improving conditions; Gradgrind's system used to humorously expose educational practices; some solution offered in greater creativity but vague and ambiguous (is Sissy supposed to be better off not being able to do maths?).
- Atwood – novel as a warning about what could happen; as a reflection of life under real oppressive regimes; consideration of problems of gender; use of flashbacks to show problems of 1980s; sense that often solutions to perceived problems do not work; some sense of rebellion providing solutions.
- Ibsen – presentation of middle-class life as oppressive for women; the effect of the norms of the society on an individual (Nora); solution presented in terms of Nora asserting her independence and leaving; ending seen as a shocking dramatic gesture rather than a solution.
- Shakespeare – ideas about the rights and wrongs of rebelling against the monarch explored but not fully solved; Henry's triumph suggests resolution, but he is not fully secure; the potential problem of Hal's unsuitability for the crown solved by his personal development.

And finally … try to look on your exams as an opportunity rather than an ordeal. You've been given two and a half or three hours in a peaceful environment to express your ideas about texts you've studied and (let's hope) enjoyed. Here are the two best pieces of advice I've ever been given about sitting exams:
- **Don't 'cram' the night before; eat properly, get some fresh air and have a good night's sleep.**
- **RTBQ (Read the Bloody Question).**